The Balancing Acts of
Academic Leadership

The Balancing Acts of Academic Leadership

A Guide for Department Chairs and Deans

Jeanne A. K. Hey

ROWMAN & LITTLEFIELD
Lanham • Boulder • New York • London

Published by Rowman & Littlefield
An imprint of The Rowman & Littlefield Publishing Group, Inc.
4501 Forbes Boulevard, Suite 200, Lanham, Maryland 20706
www.rowman.com

86-90 Paul Street, London EC2A 4NE, United Kingdom

British Library Cataloguing in Publication Information Available

Library of Congress Cataloging-in-Publication Data

Names: Hey, Jeanne A. K., author.
Title: The balancing acts of academic leadership : a guide for department chairs and deans / Jeanne A. K. Hey.
Description: Lanham : Rowman & Littlefield Publishing Group, [2021] | Includes bibliographical references. | Summary: "This book's 'leadership seesaws' break down your leadership style into a series of choice points that will help you improve your effectiveness"—Provided by publisher.
Identifiers: LCCN 2021029533 (print) | LCCN 2021029534 (ebook) | ISBN 9781475855005 (cloth) | ISBN 9781475855012 (paperback) | ISBN 9781475855029 (epub)
Subjects: LCSH: Educational leadership. | Education, Higher—Aims and objectives. | Universities and colleges—Administration.
Classification: LCC LB2806 .H49 2021 (print) | LCC LB2806 (ebook) | DDC 378.1/11—dc23
LC record available at https://lccn.loc.gov/2021029533
LC ebook record available at https://lccn.loc.gov/2021029534

To Paulette St. Ours, Charles Tilburg, Susan Gray, David Guay, and Amy Keirstead, the dream team of associate deans

Contents

Foreword

Today the development of leaders in our society is at a critical junction—too important to leave to chance. The corporate world complains of simply progressing from the Bronze Age of leadership development to the Iron Age. If this is true, I fear colleges and universities may still be in the Dark Ages. Jeanne Hey's book illuminates the way to enter the Building Age of academic leadership. Dr. Hey's primer on academic leadership gives precision and prescription to what ails deans, department chairs, and directors—their delicate balancing acts of leadership.

Jeanne Hey is an experienced academic leader, having served in the roles of dean, associate provost, and program director over her career in higher education. She also is an experienced provider of professional development programs, specializing in leadership training for department chairs, program directors, and deans. What you will find most inviting and helpful are her insights and advice. Written in the first person, you realize you have a friend in the author, who has been there before and who shares the same struggles and challenges you may be experiencing. Her writing style draws you in with her credibility as a colleague and wisdom from decades of experience.

Academic leaders (deans, department chairs, and program coordinators) typically come to the position *without* leadership training, *without* prior executive experience, *without* a clear understanding of the ambiguity and complexity of their roles, *without* recognition of the metamorphic changes that occur as one transform from an academic to an administrator, and *without* an awareness of the cost to their academic and personal lives. In essence, academic leaders are an imperiled species, suffering from an imbalance between personal and professional lives and between leadership responsibilities and academic goals. The transformation from faculty to academic leadership takes time and dedication, and not all faculty make the complete and successful transition to leadership.

The Balancing Act of Academic Leaders addresses eight professional challenges academic leaders face and strategies for how successfully to find balance. Henri Matisse once reflected: "What I dream of is an art of balance, of purity and serenity devoid of troubling or depressing subject matter . . . a soothing, calming influence on the mind, something like a good armchair which provides relaxation from . . . fatigue." In today's academy, many of us dream of balance and serenity—if not in our professions, at least in our personal lives.

Many metaphors could depict this balancing act—a tight rope, a swivel chair, a juggler. In a university commencement address, a CEO spoke of a balancing or juggling act between our personal and professional lives: Imagine life as a game, in which you are juggling some five balls in the air. You name them *work, family, health, friends,* and *spirit,* and you keep all of these in the air. You will soon understand that *work* is a rubber ball. If you drop it, it will bounce back. But the other four balls—*family, health, friends,* and *spirit*—are made of glass. If you drop one of these, they will be scuffed, marked, nicked, damaged, or even shattered. They will never be the same. Thus, he advised to strive to find balance in your life.

The author, Jeanne Hey, once considered the tightrope walker's balancing act as a metaphor but has realized that when they make a wrong decision, they are doomed or die. Academic leadership is not this dire or dichotomous, clouded in right or wrong decisions. She astutely portrays seesaws as the balancing act, not so much as hitting a single point of strength, style, identity, or comfort, but situated in the middle of two camps—for example, balancing faculty vs. administration interests. You are neither faculty nor administration but somewhere on the seesaw seeking balance between the two. Jeanne Hey's book can help you reflect and achieve this critical balance in life—and between your personal and professional challenges.

Deans, department chairs, and program directors often feel trapped between their leadership role and their former primary roles as teachers and scholars. They find themselves caught in a balancing act. Trying to look two directions, they mediate the administrative concerns but at the same time try to champion their scholarly pursuits. They find themselves balancing between their scholarship interests and their administrative responsibilities. In essence, they are caught in the role of Janus, a Roman god whose two faces look in different directions at the same time. Although deans and chairs need not worry about being deified, they do find themselves in a paradoxical position. Like no other managers, many must attend to their fiduciary responsibilities and at the same time work to protect their personal teaching and scholarly interests.

While balancing these two roles, they must find the right position on the seesaw without becoming dizzy, schizophrenic, or self-serving.

Part of this paradoxical balancing act of performing scholarly activities while attending to managerial tasks lies in the nature of managerial work: an unrelenting pace characterized by brevity, variety, and fragmentation. Academic leaders log dozens of written and verbal contacts daily peppered with drop-in visitors, text messages, and self-interruptions. They only average nine minutes of uninterrupted desk time before they are off to their next task. No wonder scholarship, for example, rarely emerges during the workday, as nine minutes is hardly enough time to germinate an idea, let alone conceptualize a strategic plan, scholarly thought, or teaching plan. Thus, the brief encounter with each activity, the variety of activities, and the lack of any activity pattern (with the exception of meetings, meetings, meetings) require leaders to shift gears quickly and frequently. In effect, they rush from one task to another, day by day and week by week, and rarely received satisfaction from completing a rewarding scholarly task. They find themselves between a rock and a hard place—caught in the crevasse between two potentially different value systems.

As a former dean, department chair, and program director for over thirty-five years, I have now returned to my roots as professor. For decades in academic administration, I struggled with two major balancing acts: (1) between my personal and professional life and (2) between my faculty and administration roles and identity. As I searched for balance, I realized that *balance* is not a noun or a destination, but a journey with multiple paths. Reading Jeanne Hey's book gave me new insights, tools, and platforms for practice I wished I had mastered while serving as a chair and dean—and husband and father. She will help you on your journey.

I highly recommend this book for not only beginning academic leaders but also all academic leaders and those still considering the call to leadership. In addition, this is a must-read for provosts and presidents, especially those who have never served, or walked in the shoes of a dean, chair, or director. They too need to read, understand, and empathize with the seesaws they may have never ridden.

Start by reading the book's introduction, as it will ground you. Then, read chapter 1 to get an overview of the eight seesaws. Then you will be ready to dive into the first balancing act you find most urgent and important to you professionally and personally. Eight seesaws may appear overwhelming, especially to new aspiring academic leaders. Some of these imbalances appear to be more structural and inherent in the position and institution. Other imbalances fall within your control as an academic leader and must be personally managed. Choose your points on the seesaw—especially in chapter 7 and 8 addressing availability and attention. You will want to manage your time and the key people on your management molecule. The book is filled with wonderful insights and advice, and the last chapter concludes with themes, lessons, and advice.

These balancing acts are never fully and truly resolved. The "right" actions will always be a matter of judgment. Becoming an astute and competent academic leader requires a lengthy—and difficult—personal journey. Swiveling between "right versus right" decisions on the seesaw requires self-knowledge, an inner and often lonely journey. It is about finding your voice and passion to serve.

Inevitably, all leaders eventually leave their positions. Is your destiny to return to faculty or on to higher levels of management? Before you leave, you may want to reflect on whether you made a difference. Answer the following question: When you leave your leadership position, what do you hope others will think you have accomplished? What will be your legacy? Do you envision a legacy that supersedes both your personal and professional lives? I surveyed over a thousand chairs and deans across the United States and Down Under in Australia. Three themes consistently emerged from their legacy statements: (1) we advanced our *programs*—our department/school is in a better place than before; (2) we advanced *people*—faculty and staff were promoted; and (3) we did it with *decency*!

IF YOU HAD TO WRITE YOUR LEGACY TODAY, WHAT WOULD IT BE?

Balancing Acts gives you precision and prescription for eight balancing acts challenging academic leaders. To recount or dwell on these eight seesaws should not deafen the call to leadership but rather calls attention to the obstacles leaders need to overcome in order to develop their latent talents and find balance in their lives. Remember, you are also a role model for potential leaders who may look to you for sage advice to advance their careers. *Pay it forward*. How can you help them clear the obstacles of a reluctant leader—to ignite their flame of servant leadership without burning out? Illuminate the morass of balancing acts academic leaders live by, and enlighten others of the challenges frequently unnoticed and often left in the dark for others to discover on their own. Ultimately, institutions of higher education will continue to have a leadership crisis if the conditions for deans, chairs, and directors remain unmanageable. The future for academic leadership may appear plagued with imbalances, but it is also replete with creative solutions and the feelings of making a difference.

Walt Gmelch
Professor of Leadership Studies and Dean Emeritus
University of San Francisco

Preface

2019

In 2019, after eight years as dean of the College of Arts and Sciences at the University of New England (UNE), I stepped down and joined the ranks of full-time faculty. Mine was a happy and atypical conclusion to a senior leadership position in academia.

Most deans complete their terms in ways other than voluntary resignation with years of employment at the same institution ahead of them. Many retire, ending their careers as dean emeriti. Others move on to become deans, provosts, and presidents at other universities. Some are promoted to those posts within their own institution. Some are forced out, either by their institution's administrators or via faculty votes of no confidence. A few resign out of unhappiness and stress.

I am among the fortunate who stepped down voluntarily while still happy in my job. I perceived that my contributions to the College of Arts and Sciences at UNE were beginning to wane and thus felt a responsibility to step aside. At the same time, I had no aspirations to become a provost or to serve at another institution. As it happens, eight years is well beyond the average tenure for an academic dean, which falls between three and five years, depending on one's field.[1] More importantly, it also lies on the outer edge of when most deans remain creative and effective.[2]

Because I work in higher education, my decision to resign my post entailed none of the negative consequences that it would in nearly all other employment sectors. When most individuals abandon their leadership position, they have no choice but to leave that company or organization entirely. A decision to leave leadership usually means a concurrent decision to face the transition to a new place of employment. Such a transition is often filled with uncertainty and risk. In contrast, we academic leaders enjoy many benefits, even in resigning.

Most obvious among these is the fact that I still had a secure and tenured position awaiting me in the faculty. I now carry the lofty-

sounding title of "dean emerita." I enjoyed a semester-long sabbati-
cal, during which I wrote most of this book. Some deans even retain
their dean's salary when they return to teaching and scholarship.
Finally, and perhaps most satisfying, I am able to observe and enjoy
the successes of an academic unit that I worked so hard to build and
grow during my years as dean. In my particular case, administrative work eventually returned to my portfolio; after a year in the
faculty, I transitioned to splitting my time between positions as a
faculty member and associate provost.

Why do I begin this book on academic leadership with my decision to *leave* my leadership position? First, because it illustrates a
truth that I hope to share with readers: academic leadership positions—program directors, department heads, deans—are too often
thought of as painful service rather than as the career and happiness
boosters they can be. I am not alone in discovering myriad joys and
benefits emerging from the experience of higher-ed leadership. That
one can *leave* such a position with nearly no negative career consequences and with many advantages highlights that truth.

Second, the conclusion of my deanship provided me with both
the experience and the time to collect my thoughts, observations,
and lessons learned from years in the trenches. My mistakes, successes, missteps, and achievements all combine into a knowledge
and skillset that would have benefited me immensely when I
started the job.

Like nearly every other department head and dean, I took on
leadership positions with next to no training in how to approach,
much less perform, the tasks assigned. The credentials I brought to
these posts,[3] and the ones on which search committees assessed me,
lay largely in the areas of teaching and scholarship. Once I became
dean, I set aside teaching and research to focus on leadership, management, strategic planning, and running the day-to-day operations
of a college. It remains an enduring irony that the basis on which
academic candidates are measured has little to do with the actual
leadership tasks and responsibilities they take on.

The nearly wholesale absence of training for academic leaders—
especially new department and program heads who are first-timers
in leadership positions—not only discourages many promising candidates from seeking the position but also undermines their effectiveness once they assume the post.

This book, then, is aimed both at *encouraging* you to consider
academic leadership as a career choice and at *training* you in elements of success. In short, this is a book for aspiring, new, and

current academic leaders. It is the type of book I wish I'd had when I started climbing the leadership ranks in higher education.

The complexity and number of challenges, opportunities, crises, roadblocks, and demands facing academic leaders can feel overwhelming. You are accountable to many and varied constituencies—college presidents, provosts, deans, faculty, students, parents, community leaders, and more. These same individuals and groups often demand contradictory decisions, policy, and actions. The president and provost, for example, may push you to cut an expensive and underenrolled program. The faculty and students in that program will resist such a move publicly and vociferously.

These constant and contrasting demands make many leaders feel squeezed into a box with few choices that will please all or even most of the people surrounding them. That box can be a lonely place, especially if you lack the training and skillset to handle it, much less a strong support system to provide perspective and encouragement.

Furthermore, nearly all of the people who want or need something from you will provide advice on how you should behave. The president may say, "You must be more decisive." The faculty counter, "You must be more transparent." Students want you to be student-focused, while the board of trustees demands financial accountability. A provost may expect you to be deeply engaged in the workings of your units, while those units' faculty criticize you as a micromanager.

Too many leaders, and those who advise them, seek out the *individual qualities* that make a good leader. As the above examples demonstrate, those qualities often oppose each other. What faculty see as transparency and good listening are interpreted as indecisiveness and inaction by the president.

The constant test is not to find the single correct approach, but to find the proper balance among the many competing leadership choices facing you. This concept sounds simple but is challenging to put into effect. This book provides you a series of frameworks to achieve it.

If you read nothing other than this preface, then, take away this message: effective leadership relies not on a *static* series of personal attributes, tactics, and decisions, but rather on one's ability to *adapt* to the situation at hand with a wide variety of attributes, tactics, and decisions. Happily, adaptability is a skill you can learn and develop.

2020 ARRIVES

When I took on this book project in 2019, the trials facing department heads, deans, provosts, and presidents had already surpassed anything experienced before. Public colleges and universities in the United States had struggled with more than two decades of state and federal budget cuts. Demographic shifts, especially in the Northeast and Midwest, created enrollment challenges for all but the most elite schools and threatened many others' veritable existence. The cost to provide students with a twenty-first-century college education was rising at a higher rate than institutions' ability to raise revenue. Conversations and controversies about everything from shared governance to curriculum to college budgets to racism and sexual assault on campus rocked relationships among faculty, students, and administrators.

Into these sea-changing times dropped COVID-19 and with it the closure of almost all college and university doors overnight in March 2020. A few months later came George Floyd's murder and the surge of Black Lives Matter protests and renewed calls for dramatic societal change. These events put important demands on university presidents and their teams; many demonstrated impressive leadership around them. Many others were rebuked for their failure to respond sufficiently to systemic racism in the academy. The subsequent months and semesters saw academic leaders manage challenges that were literally unimaginable before that moment. Nearly every challenge they were already struggling with—stressed financial resources, tense administration-faculty relationships, poor graduation rates—magnified. In most cases, those same leaders implemented a salary freeze, and in some cases salary and workforce reductions.

The pandemic hit at exactly the moment that I returned full time to a faculty position, and thus complicated my adjustment to teaching, scholarship, and faculty service after many years in administration. Amidst my pandemic concerns stood a particularly stark challenge: cancer. My college-aged son arrived home for the December holiday of his sophomore year not feeling well. We soon learned he suffered from an aggressive form of leukemia, one with a multiyear treatment protocol, a likelihood of serious complications, and a very real risk of death. As I write this, he has just passed his first anniversary since diagnosis and is soldiering forward.

Although my own family's medical news is dire, it does not cause particularly atypical challenges. Within almost every professional's life comes that unexpected, or even expected, event that takes one's attention away from work, one's time away from the office, and one's ability to be available around the clock away from them. These same events recalibrate our sense of what matters most in life and reframe where our academic leadership job fits into that calculation.

Anyone contemplating or serving in a leadership position in such a cauldron of change and distress faces a daunting prospect, for sure. At the same time, higher education is in greater need of individuals to join the senior administrative ranks than ever. Nearly everything about the "traditional" model of higher education in the United States is experiencing scrutiny and pressure to change. Institutions can no longer raise tuition without regard for inflation or families' ability to pay. A demographic "time bomb" is set to hit in 2025, at which point 15% fewer new students will enter post-secondary educational institutions than in the previous generation.[4] The American population's confidence in higher education's capacity to perform its role efficiently and effectively is waning.[5] News stories about coddled professors abusing the privileges of tenure abound, while fewer and fewer tenure-track faculty comprise the teaching ranks.[6]

How does Higher Education hope to address, much less overcome, these challenges without supremely dedicated, capable, and well-trained leaders? It cannot. My hope is that faculty members who read this book will feel encouraged to take the leap into leadership, and that aspiring and current leaders will continue to grow and take on new positions. I can think of few higher causes than contributing to the stewardship of one of the world's most honorable institutions.

I encourage you to use this book as your companion on your academic leadership journey. The leadership balancing acts you explore here can act as a long-lasting support system to which you can return time and again to orient your decision-making and leadership choices.

Companions, friends, colleagues, mentors, family members, and those who display random acts of kindness are all essential elements of any leader's support system. When you take on a role in the higher levels of academic leadership, you immediately become vulnerable to criticism, some of it misinformed, widely distributed, and even cruel. Rely on those close to you and those who understand the many challenges you face.

The people who play that role in my life are far too many to mention. To create such a list not only would make for a very long chapter but also would invite the chance of omitting someone important. So I will acknowledge here only two of the many dozens of individuals who helped bring me to a place where I could write this volume.

Mary Woodworth became my mentor when I began to envision a future in the administrative ranks of academia. A highly accomplished microbiologist and cancer researcher, Mary served as chair of microbiology and then as associate provost at Miami University for many years. She provided excellent and clear advice, warned me when I was in danger of committing an error, and nominated and advocated for me to take on important leadership roles in the university. She paved the way for me to gain the experience necessary to later land a deanship. I am forever in her debt.

I acknowledge Owen Hey because he has endured a very serious diagnosis and associated treatments with such grace and perseverance. What could have upended our family, not to mention my work, has instead brought us closer together. He has shown extraordinary fortitude in the face of a disease that not only disrupts his formative years but also threatens his life. He nonetheless remains one of my greatest cheerleaders. It is an honor and a humbling experience to be his mother.

NOTES

1. Indeed, vice presidents of academic affairs in the United States enjoy a median tenure of only 3.5 years, well below that of university presidents and all other vice presidents and senior directors, including of financial affairs, development, student affairs, athletics, human resources, registrar, and facilities. CUPA-HR, "2017–18 Administrators in Higher Education Survey" (College and University Professional Association for Human Resources, 2018).

2. Walter H. Gmelch, D. Hopkins, and S. Damico, Seasons of a Dean's Life (Sterling, VA: Stylus, 2011).

3. I served as a program head for nine years and interim campus dean and executive director for one year at Miami University before moving to UNE.

4. Missy Kline, "The Looming Higher Ed Enrollment Cliff," *Higher Ed Magazine*, 2009.

5. Doug Lederman, "The Public's Support for (and Doubts about) Higher Ed," *Inside Higher Ed*, June 17, 2019.

6. LaMont Jones, "Growing Proportion of Part-Time Faculty Portends Problems," *Diverse*, July 11, 2019.

Introduction

Embrace Your Leadership!

"WELCOME TO YOUR LEADERSHIP POSITION?"

"Congratulations on being appointed department chair! Or should I say 'condolences'?" As an academic leader, you have no doubt heard this refrain repeatedly from faculty colleagues. The speaker invariably thinks, and probably intends, it to be a good-natured joke.

The subtext, however, is clear: "Good for you for taking on this job, but we both know it won't be a rewarding experience." In this way, academic leaders are welcomed into their new positions less with excitement and genuine felicitations than with expressions of regret. What an unhappy way to begin a new leadership opportunity!

This tiny window into academic life illustrates an imbedded culture in which faculty approach their institutional leaders with an *a priori* posture of distrust, suspicion, and even disdain. Their greatest mistrust is directed toward leaders from units outside of academic affairs (e.g., college presidents, chief financial officers, vice presidents of student affairs, chief strategy officers). But even those very leaders whose careers began and were formed in the faculty ranks become targets of mistrust as soon as they take on a leadership position, such as chair, program director, or dean. They have passed, as we say, to the *dark side*.[1]

I gained a glimpse into this culture very early in my own academic career. I was a graduate student, earning my PhD in political science at a major research university. I befriended an assistant professor in a department different from my own. She was not only a friend but also a role model, as I hoped to follow the faculty path on which she had recently embarked herself.

One day I mentioned to her, "I think I might want to go into administration someday." She looked at me with a horrified expression, as if I had said something along the lines of "I think I might

1

want to torture children someday." Her response: "I think you have too much character and integrity for that." She meant it as a compliment. But her comment confused me, because the idea that administrators lacked character and integrity had not occurred to me.

In that moment I learned a lesson that had somehow escaped me in my young academic journey: many faculty operate from an assumption that administrators are the bad guys, the sell-outs, the opposition. It is a lesson I had to learn, and an obstacle I had to overcome, repeatedly, over my years as a faculty member and then as an academic leader.

It is important to acknowledge, of course, that the "faculty vs. administration" trope is not universally embraced. To discuss American higher education's culture in broad strokes necessarily misses the many differences across institutions. Some colleges and universities enjoy a healthy and trusting relationship between faculty and administration. And many members of the faculty welcome new academic leaders with positivity and encouragement.

Indeed, *most* faculty want to see their chairs, deans, provosts, and presidents succeed. On an individual level, faculty members typically interact with their leaders in friendly and productive ways. Even in their most critical moments, their intent is to engage in productive and positive ways.

Similarly, some criticism directed at administrators is well earned. American higher education has its share of genuinely bad leaders who execute poor decisions or approach their leadership as much as a vehicle for personal advancement as for institutional mission and success. Furthermore, faculty are essential partners in shared governance. They enjoy a valid and necessary role in decision-making and in checking excessive exercise of institutional power.

These healthy and necessary faculty checks on administrative power notwithstanding, higher education has developed a *culture*, so ingrained that it often goes unnoticed, that paints administrators and faculty as natural antagonists, rather than as members of a larger team working toward a common interest. And because administration is associated with decision-making authority, administrators receive faculty's mistrust and, too often, their scorn. Some administrators thus confront an atmosphere of suspicion from day one, long before most of them commit any specific errors harmful enough to earn the faculty's legitimate criticism.

We should not be surprised, then, that a faculty member, upon being named department chair or dean, is greeted with condolences as much as with congratulations. It is nonetheless sad and unnecessary. The "us vs. them" culture does significant damage—to shared governance, to decision-making effectiveness, and equally importantly, to the professional satisfaction and success of those faculty who do take on leadership positions.

Academia *needs* leaders. It needs strong, enthusiastic deans and department heads who enjoy the support not just of their presidents and provosts but also of their faculty and students. In this moment of great upheaval and enormous challenge in American higher education, wise leadership is essential not only to institutional success but also to many institutions' very survival.

Faculty benefit immensely from the work of effective leaders who engage in everything from the day-to-day departmental logistics to managing difficult people and problems. An effective chair completes the multitude of administrative tasks necessary to keep a department running, allowing faculty to focus on teaching, advising, and scholarship.

Furthermore, a good chair does not act alone, but creates the conditions under which a department becomes more than the sum of its parts. She brings together each individual's contributions and point of view to generate a collective vision and a plan to execute it. These are demanding tasks that, when performed well, make a department a joyous place to work and a productive center for student and faculty achievement. Yet too few of our program directors and department chairs obtain the appreciation and recognition they deserve. And far too few are encouraged to think of academic leadership as the noble professional pursuit that it is.

MYTHS AND ASSUMPTIONS

Certainly no faculty member who delivers the "or should I say 'condolences'" line intends to hurt a new chair's feelings. So why does he say it? A series of assumptions underlie this seemingly blithe remark (and its "you've gone to the dark side" cousin). These assumptions merit scrutiny, for they frequently make faculty who aspire to leadership feel that they have to apologize for doing so.

The flipside of the "condolences" script is the equally common refrain from academic leaders themselves: "I never wanted to be chair." Although this is no doubt true for some academic leaders, many protest a bit too much, as if trying to convince the listener that their leadership position is accidental, performed under duress, anything but deliberate or planned. A careful look at the assumptions that paint the leadership position as undesirable at best, and a traitorous power grab at worst, also reveals the many myths surrounding what academic leadership positions are really like.

Myth: The Chair's Job Stinks

What lies underneath the "or should I say condolences" thinking? First, many faculty operate with the impression that the department head's job is thankless, difficult, onerous, and not much fun. They may have heard chairs complain about the tasks, the time commitment, the difficult people, the administration.

No doubt there are too many institutions where this unhappy portrait is accurate, where chairs shoulder too many burdens and enjoy too few joys and opportunities. Where they receive little appreciation from students, faculty, and senior leadership. Where the maxim "No good deed goes unpunished" frequently sums up their day at work.

Let it be clearly stated that this description applies to genuinely *dysfunctional* work environments. Those suffering in such situations should work with colleagues and leaders to change them. And faculty are right to avoid serving as leaders within such cultures.

Let it also be stated that such thoroughly dysfunctional cultures are rare. Certainly, deans, chairs, and directors suffer their share of tough days in which difficult people, maddening bureaucracy, and too many meetings make for an unpleasant experience. Many find that they are objectively busier that they were before taking the position.

But these leaders also enjoy opportunities, pleasures, and perquisites. They have the privilege of directing their department toward greater success. They celebrate faculty and student achievements. They have enhanced access to the dean and provost. They experience the appreciation of students and their families whose lives have changed as a result of their work. They enjoy the greater schedule flexibility that comes with course release, and with the authority to schedule one's own courses. Most also earn a salary boost. They discover their talents in leadership and administration.

These are but a few of the many benefits of academic leadership. Few chairs are willing to talk about them. To do so invites the scorn of others who look askance at anyone who "enjoys" leadership in the academy. Instead, they complain about how busy they are, grumble about tiresome meetings, anything but rejoice in how satisfied and fulfilled they feel in the leadership position.

Lesson: The chair's job can be rewarding and fun.

Myth: Chairs and Program Directors Necessarily Forfeit Their Research Success, and Promotion Prospects, to the Demands of Leadership

Many faculty eschew leadership, believing that being department head means an end to their research productivity. Assistant and associate professors are told that becoming chair means a delay in their promotion and the salary and job-security benefits that accompany it. Indeed, "chairs get no research done" has gained truth-statement status in the academy, no longer questioned or even examined. And of course there are too many cases in which it is true. However, as with the "the chair's job stinks" proclamation, it doesn't have to be that way, and in many cases, it simply is not.

Upon reflection and after a look around their campus, most academics acknowledge that many associate and even some assistant professors who act as department chairs succeed in their promotions to the next level, often without delay. Those chairs share two factors that support their success.

First, they prioritize their scholarship, not to the detriment of their teaching and leadership duties, but on equal footing with them. By staying true to their priorities, they carve out time and energy for research. Second, they operate in a culture that supports their career trajectory. Their deans and provosts value their work as chairs, teachers, *and* scholars. They continue to enjoy enough schedule flexibility to dedicate time blocks to scholarship, often aided by course release.

My own story as an associate professor named program director is instructive here. In my third year as a tenured associate professor of political science and international studies, the international studies program directorship vacated. The opening came earlier than I thought ideal, given that I was fairly recently tenured and parenting two small children, one who was still nursing. I nonetheless dove into the opportunity without much thought as to its potential effects on my future promotion.

I am forever thankful to the dean of arts and sciences, who offered me the position. He told me he had great confidence in my leadership capacities and looked forward to seeing the program thrive under my direction. "But," he warned, "do not let this position be an obstacle to your getting promoted. Keep your eye on that prize."

I had shared the common goal of a research career dedicated to answering our discipline's most pressing questions through circuitous paths filled with stops and starts, successes and failures, journal acceptances and rejections. My dean's counsel urged me to laser-focus on keeping my scholarship on track, and to not allow the seemingly endless tasks of program leadership to overwhelm my time. I earned promotion to professor a few years later.

My story is more common than many think. It is an example of one person's success in *both* leadership and scholarly output when she enjoyed the two factors described above. My university supported my dedication to my research program, and I maintained scholarship as a professional priority even after becoming director. Was I busier than before? Yes, absolutely. But I also embarked on a highly rewarding path of academic leadership and am very glad that I did not wait to do so.

Lesson: Becoming a department or program leader does not require you to sacrifice your research and promotion prospects.

Assumption: A Chair Who "Thinks Like an Administrator" Is Dangerous to Faculty Interests

Colleagues who discourage you from taking on the chair because they worry about your being overworked or sacrificing your scholarship may be poorly informed, but they likely have your best interests in mind. There is another, and less charitable, motivation behind the "dark side" and "condolences" comments, however.

When a faculty member suggests that you have gone to the dark side, even in jest, he gives voice to the notion that administrators are untrustworthy and acting in opposition to faculty interests, a myth I denounce earlier in this chapter. He is telling you not to imagine that you have real authority over him, that you best not consider yourself the boss, and that you better take his side in cases in which faculty and administration interests diverge. The meta-message is "I support you in running the department, attending meetings, and writing annual evaluations. But don't think you can tell me what to do."

Faculty rightly value their independence and academic freedom. Any leader who treads on these commits a mistake. But sometimes faculty interpret their independence as freedom from contributing to department and university strategic directions, participation in events, adjusting their courses to fit the departmental curricular decisions, and so forth.

Some imagine that the chair is a department clerk, responsible for paperwork, meetings, and deadlines, but without any real authority or strategic responsibilities. This group views the faculty body not as a professional collective with a common mission, but as a group of independent contractors dedicated to largely individual pursuits while working on the same campus.

Faculty who take this view err in three important ways. First, the chair-as-clerk image conforms with very few real job descriptions. The vast majority of universities endow chairs with decision-making authority, supervisory oversight, and strategic responsibilities. They are not the paper pushers and function attenders some old-fashioned notions imagine. Chairs have the duty to behave like real leaders, whether their faculty recognize it or not.

Second, a department cannot thrive without genuinely empowered leadership. An effective chair leads the unit to become more than the sum of its parts. This demands visionary thinking, skilled management, and honest evaluation of faculty performance. Some faculty chafe at the idea that they have a "boss," but most celebrate when a strong chair has steered the department toward greater achievement.

Third, the outdated model of academics operating independently, largely left alone by department chairs who focus on administrative tasks, simply no longer works. Most colleges and universities today face enormous and even existential challenges: shrinking enrollments, rising costs, declining state support, increasing demands from students and their families, growing outrage about student debt, and so on.

A laissez-faire approach to department leadership cannot possibly meet all of these challenges. They demand an engaged, strategic, and unified approach by all members of the department. Anything less risks the department's success and even survival. We read about such departments on a regular basis. They are downsized, merged with others, and eliminated. We no longer live in an age in which academic departments can afford to avoid effective leadership.

Similarly outdated, then, is the idea that a department chair should act primarily as a faculty advocate to the administration, the latter presumed to be the adversary. Instead, department faculty are wise to promote chairs who not only enjoy positive relationships with senior leadership but also spend time thinking like an administrator—that is, strategizing about how to respond to new challenges, situate the department for growth, spend limited funds more productively, and increase student enrollments.

Dedication to these issues does not mean that the chair cannot and should not also promote faculty interests, such as arguing for salary increases, enhanced research space, and a strong faculty voice in university decision-making. In today's environment, an effective chair pays strong attention to both of these roles.

Lesson: Chairs who see themselves as administrators are a benefit to faculty interests.

EMBRACE YOUR LEADERSHIP

This book calls on faculty members to resist the culture that discourages them from aspiring to leadership. It urges department chairs and program directors to discover and enjoy the confidence that comes with an important job well done.

Rather than apologize for your leadership, celebrate it! Don't give in to the voice telling you to complain about how busy and stressed you are. Instead, broadcast that you are grateful for this chance to serve your program and the university. When a colleague says to you, "Congratulations, or should I say 'condolences'?" respond immediately with "Definitely 'congratulations'! I'm really excited for the opportunity." When another speaks in a way that vilifies administrators, remind her that you are an administrator now and are proud to be part of the leadership team.

In other words, *embrace* your leadership. Embrace it as an opportunity to grow professionally, advance your career, earn a higher salary, and most importantly, lead your department and college to a better future.

I have shared this recommendation with hundreds of current and future department chairs. At first, most respond with disbelief. Their faces reveal that such an idea had never occurred to them. But quickly, most become excited about the prospect that they can be an academic leader and actually love their job. I encourage you to imagine that possibility, and then to make it so.

An interesting thing happens when a department chair or program director stops apologizing for and instead embraces his leadership position. The faculty who value his work and appreciate his leadership (nearly always the majority) become more visible and more vocal. The joy that comes from working in a department led by an able, strategic, and strong individual over time drowns out the disparagers' "dark side" voices (usually a small minority). The culture that, in ways both subtle and overt, devalues "administration" is replaced by one that celebrates excellent leadership as much as it does excellent teaching and scholarship.

Academic leadership is never easy. Few of us have any training in it. We typically work in cultures that do too little to support and recognize program directors, department chairs, and deans. Our daily tasks involve many difficult situations, including department bullies, failing technology, and shrinking budgets. All of this is true. This picture, however, excludes all the benefits of academic leadership that deserve as much attention as the pitfalls.

The remainder of this book is dedicated to helping chairs, directors, and deans enhance their leadership effectiveness. More important than any individual piece of advice or strategy to manage a particular situation is this introduction's theme: *embrace your leadership.*

When academic leaders allow themselves to own their authority, without apology, excuse, or embarrassment, not only do they find greater professional satisfaction, but they also become better at their jobs. It takes a lot of emotional energy to perform all the tasks of leadership when your colleagues downplay the very value of your position. When you abandon the negativity around your role, you enjoy more time and energy to dedicate to the job. Embracing your leadership is a form of self-empowerment that also rubs off on others. When faculty see *you* celebrating the importance of academic leadership, they will begin to question their own flawed assumptions about the so-called "dark side."

ESSENTIAL IDEAS IN THIS CHAPTER

- Faculty work in an environment that often disdains administrative and leadership work.
- An "us vs. them" culture that pits faculty and administration against each other is harmful, unnecessary, and often inconsistent with the realities of shared interests.
- Academic leaders and those aspiring to leadership should resist the negative connotations associated with "the administration" and instead embrace their leadership goals and positions.

- Many myths about leadership positions wrongly keep faculty from applying for the department chair, program director, associate dean, or dean.

NOTE

1. Richard Castallo describes well the faculty culture within which university leaders operate; see Richard T. Castallo, *Dealing with Dysfunction: A Book for University Leaders* (Boulder: Rowman and Littlefield, 2017).

ONE

The Seesaws of Academic Leadership

A Framework for Fine-Tuning Your Leadership Choices

Imagine a group of faculty who ask, "What makes a great academic leader?" Responses would include "decisive," "inclusive," "humble," "intelligent," "data-driven," "transparent," "visionary," "grounded in values," "confident," "detail-oriented," "ethical," and "good listener." A person endowed with these traits would likely make an effective leader. But does such a person exist? Especially given that a number of these very descriptors are opposites of each other?

Few excel at being *both* visionary and detail-oriented, for example. When a leader acts decisively, his critics decry his lack of transparency. One who exudes confidence rarely also projects humility. Today, a leader is celebrated for being grounded in values; tomorrow she is derided for not acting in a sufficiently data-driven way. It is not impossible to exhibit all these qualities, but it is difficult, especially in higher education where leadership training is so lacking.

The list is wise, nonetheless, because it points to a truism: effective leaders must demonstrate all of these qualities, and many more. Rather than being defined by singular traits—strong, decisive, transparent, humble—leaders should employ the approach and

11

skills appropriate to the challenge, problem, or individual facing them at the moment. *They must tailor their leadership to the situation.*

Hersey and colleagues began an enduring discussion on situational leadership decades ago.[1] Heifetz similarly discusses contingent and adaptive leadership.[2] What seems obvious—that different situations call for different leadership approaches—is too often forgotten when universities seek out leaders.

Rare is the job advertisement for a new department head, dean, provost, or president stating that the university seeks someone with the "ability to fluctuate their leadership style and to bring a diverse set of tools to each problem and opportunity."

Rather, they seek out leaders who are "strong, visionary, transparent, committed to the liberal arts," and many other traits that, though desirable, likely scare off some would-be applicants who imagine it impossible to check off every box on the list. This is unfortunate. The essential quality for a successful leader is not an individual trait, but rather the ability to identify which leadership choices fit the moment.

This book provides current and aspiring academic leaders with an instrument to help you tailor your leadership to the issue at hand. It will aid you in identifying your leadership comfort zones and default settings. It then encourages you to build on these to develop a skillset that allows you to employ not only your natural approach but also the *best-suited* approach for the occasion.

No one is a perfect leader, equally strong in every possible leadership trait. Each brings his experience, training, personality, and mindset to the position. An effective leader is abundantly self-aware of these and then committed to growing in those areas in which he has deficits, doubts, and inexperience. Most importantly, he approaches each situation with deliberate thought and planning about which leadership tools he uses.

In other words, leaders must manage a *balancing act* among often-competing tactics. The balancing-act metaphor summons an image of a tight-rope walker constantly adjusting to maintain equilibrium. This contrasts with more common leadership metaphors defined by individual characteristics—for example, trail blazer, chief cheerleader, ship's captain. Each of these and all others like them suggest a static definition of what makes a good leader: someone who is grounded in a trait rather than balancing many.

The truth is that sometimes leaders have to be strong, be thick-skinned, and even cut people off. Other times they have to show vulnerability, express sensitivity, and draw on exceptional listening skills. Like the tight-rope walker, they must constantly adjust to the winds and vibrations all around them. It's a *balance*.

Although on some days, academic leaders feel as if they are walking a tightrope, rarely do we engage in the tight-rope walker's life-and-death decisions. A better metaphor for our purposes, then, is the *seesaw*, an always-moving apparatus that demands the user's constant attention. But unlike on a tightrope, when she falls off, she can get back on and try again.

THE SEESAWS OF ACADEMIC LEADERSHIP

This book introduces eight seesaws to help fine-tune your leadership decisions. Each represents a continuum of choices along a common dimension. Choosing the correct point on that continuum means properly tailoring your approach to the situation at hand. When you choose your points on the seesaws' ranges correctly, you achieve a successful *balancing act*. An overview of the seesaws illustrates the book's design.

Seesaw #1: Professional Identity

Your professional identity not only represents how you think about your own work but also influences how you project your priorities and allegiances to others. Nearly all academic leaders begin (and sometimes finish) their careers in the faculty ranks. They strongly identify as faculty and carry that identity into their work as

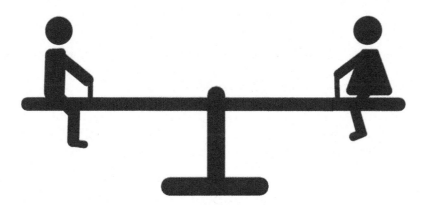

Figure 1.1. Think of Your Leadership Choices as a Balancing Act

department chairs, program directors, and deans. Yet taking on a leadership position requires that you not only act as, but also *identify as*, a member of the campus leadership team. Successful academic leaders shift between these identities depending on the challenges and opportunities they face in the moment.

Seesaw #2: Professional Role, or Whose Team Am I On?

Too often, department heads and deans are made to feel as if they must choose between advocating for the faculty and serving the administration. The reality is that they should and will do both throughout their tenure in leadership. Calls for leaders to be a "faculty advocate" are common and give rise to the myth that they must choose between playing on the "faculty team" and the "administrative team."

In fact, the administration and faculty share common interests in the vast majority of occasions. Nonetheless, many academic leaders feel pressure to play for one side or the other, often owing to the "us vs. them" culture described throughout this book. The advocate-versus-team-player seesaw helps you discern when to play these respective roles. It also reveals that in most cases, you can take a win-win approach.

Seesaw #3: Leadership Comfort Zone

American higher education is famous, or perhaps infamous, for placing promising faculty into leadership positions without so much as a formal orientation, much less appropriate leadership training. This is especially true for department chairs and program directors, but not uncommon for deans and provosts as well. What most discover is that the position requires oversight of everything from scheduling courses to strategic planning, from ordering supplies to hiring and firing staff. Understanding your strengths in these different areas is critical to your success.

The leadership-comfort-zone seesaw examines your predispositions in the myriad skillsets required of academic leaders. Where do you feel most comfortable and competent? In the trenches, ensuring that the trains run on time? Or in the visionary space, leading your unit to a better future five, ten, and twenty years from now? Your proclivities toward either end of this seesaw influence how you spend your time and your eventual impact on the department's success.

Seesaw #4: Decision-Making Style

Newly appointed academic leaders discover that their unit has a decision-making culture, a.k.a., "the way things are done." Sometimes the decision-making rules are codified in a public document. More typically, they are not, but rather they have evolved over time and are passed down through the generations.

Similarly, each individual leader develops a preference toward a particular decision-making style. The fourth seesaw asks leaders to examine both their unit's culture and their own personal inclinations as a means of enhancing decision-making effectiveness and efficiency within the unit.

This seesaw varies from centralized to democratic. In the former, decision-making is concentrated in the leader's office. In the latter, decisions are made by faculty consensus or vote. An academic unit is never served well by an approach that either is totally centralized in the chair's office or takes every decision to the faculty body. Instead, leaders must determine the issues that require genuine faculty input and distinguish those from others best decided by the head or a small group.

Seesaw #5: Management Style

Academic leaders are managers. That is, they supervise, direct, coordinate, and evaluate those who report to them. Some are chairs of small departments, supervising three or four faculty and a shared administrative assistant. Others are deans of massive schools, overseeing a complex web of assistant deans, department chairs, program directors, diverse professional staff, and a large faculty. In both cases, and in every situation in between, academic leaders must perform the delicate task of managing a group of independently minded people in a setting characterized by the absence of strict hierarchies.

The management-style seesaw asks you whether you situate yourself as the boss or as a colleague, or even a friend. The fact that department chairs and deans emerge from faculty and typically return to faculty generates special challenges for them. To be both an equal within the group and also the leader responsible for decisions is a tricky balancing act. You are at once a colleague to and supervisor of those you serve and lead.

Seesaw #6: Availability

How do you manage your office availability? "By appointment only" or "open door"? What about your electronic availability? Do you respond to email immediately, no matter when it arrives? Or do you restrict your email responses to particular times of the day and week? Many academic leaders make assumptions around availability expectations that are neither necessary nor productive.

Leaders' availability practices send important messages about their accessibility, but also about how they use and value their own time. They also sometimes unwittingly broadcast implicit expectations about how *others* manage their own availability and responsiveness. If the chair sends emails at 3:00 a.m., for example, the department's administrative assistant may assume that he is expected to respond in kind. Deliberately evaluating, and then formulating, your availability practices can have immensely positive impacts on your productivity and leadership effectiveness.

Seesaw #7: Focus of Attention

Do you direct your attention to the problems in need of remediation or to the successes that deserve celebration and reinforcement? Who earns the lion's share of your time and effort: the silent types or the squeaky wheels? Problems and squeaky wheels often earn more of their share of leaders' attention, too often at the expense of the quiet folks and the unit's achievements.

The focus-of-attention seesaws ask you to examine and adjust the balance you strike between problems and successes, squeaky wheels and silent types. A respected and effective leader cannot afford to ignore any of these and risks danger by focusing too much on any one category.

Seesaw #8: Feedback

Among the most important duties academic leaders have is evaluation of faculty and staff. Yet academia fails to train department heads and deans in the careful art of effective personnel appraisal. As a result, far too many institutions lack robust, accurate, and meaningful performance assessments.

High-impact leaders understand their role in providing formal and informal evaluation throughout the academic year. The feedback seesaws examine both the *content* and the *frequency* of a leader's assessment of faculty and staff. The content seesaw ranges from criticism to praise. The frequency seesaw ranges from abundant to almost nonexistent. Different individuals and circumstances require varied types and frequencies of feedback from you.

Ensuing chapters examine each of these in turn. There is no "ideal" or "best" place to situate yourself on any of the seesaws. Rather, you will learn to adjust the balance on each dimension to tailor your leadership to the situation at hand. Your responsibility is to approach each occasion with careful thought and deliberate choosing of the best manner in which to tackle the issue. Doing so enhances your chances of success in the moment and builds your reputation as an effective and careful leader in the long term.

ESSENTIAL IDEAS IN THIS CHAPTER

- Colleges and universities demand that their leaders demonstrate excellence in an impossibly abundant, and sometimes contradictory, number of professional traits.
- The truly most important trait for effective academic leaders is their ability to tailor their approach to the problem or opportunity at hand.
- The seesaw, or balancing act, is a useful metaphor for academic leaders facing complex issues that require them to strike the proper balance among competing interests and needs.
- This book presents eight leadership balancing acts to aid leaders in designing finely tuned strategies to meet the challenges and opportunities they face.

NOTES

1. Paul Hersey, Kenneth H. Blanchard, and Dewey E. Johnson, *Management of Organizational Behavior*, 10th ed. (New York: Pearson, 2012).

2. Ronald Heifetz, *Leadership without Easy Answers* (Cambridge: Harvard University Press, 1994).

TWO

Professional Identity

"Who am I in my professional life?" This is the essential question that determines one's professional identity. It speaks to the deeply embedded notions we use to define our work, our value, and our duties to ourselves and to all who work with us. It is often the concept that makes us most proud, for example, "I'm a *teacher*," or "I'm a *researcher*." You can also think of your identity as your professional mission, for example, "I shape young people's lives," or "I navigate my college through turbulent times."

You may not have overtly defined your professional identity before, but you surely have cultivated at least one and likely multiple professional identities. If you have not previously taken time to consider it, do so before you begin a leadership position within the academy.

Nearly all department chairs, program directors, and academic deans start their academic careers as faculty. Most chairs and directors lead the same faculty body from which they came, and to which they will return after their term ends. Having "grown up" in the faculty and forged their professional identity there, academic leaders remain deeply connected to their sense of self as a faculty member first and foremost.

Department faculty members typically encourage their chair's faculty-oriented identity. It helps to ensure that the chair will put faculty interests first and perceive institutional issues through a faculty lens.

Yet when a faculty member assumes a leadership position, she necessarily assumes a second identity—that of a leader and part of the administration. Unfortunately, few orientation sessions or other right-of-passage activities involve deliberate conversations about the meaning of this new role for its holder's sense of identity. How do I balance my role as faculty and chair? Can I perform all my leadership duties if I think of myself as faculty first and foremost? If I think of myself as a leader, will that betray my faculty alliances?

These are important questions that every department head and dean confront eventually, and it is best to consider them intentionally early in your term. New chairs are robbed of this opportunity too often because the us-versus-them culture urges them to maintain a "faculty-only" professional identity. Indeed, department chairs commonly remind their colleagues that "I am faculty first," seemingly to make sure faculty cannot accuse them of moving to the dark side.

Some academic leaders assume a strong "leadership" identity from the start. This is most common among deans and department heads who are hired from outside the institution. Especially for chairs and program directors, institutions typically look extramurally when a program is in peril or when no existing faculty are willing or able to take on the challenge. In those cases, provosts and presidents seek out someone with an explicit sense of leadership mission, so the successful candidate projects that identity.

Deans, chairs, and program directors must continually play a delicate balancing act around their professional identity as *both* leaders and faculty members. Whereas you likely arrive to the leadership position with one side of the identity seesaw more fully developed than the other, you will need to grow your awareness and expression of the other to be successful. And you will need to draw on both of those identities as you approach a staggering array of challenges, opportunities, and audiences.

Growing and expressing an identity that does not come naturally can be difficult. Especially for those who have a strong faculty identity, and who may carry a distrust of "administrators," the idea of identifying as part of the leadership may come as a challenge. If you continually project a single professional identity, you will alienate some of your constituencies. A dean may lose confidence in a chair who seems incapable of embracing her identity as a leader. Faculty members may grow suspicious of a program director who always talks like an administrator and does not appear to understand the faculty point of view. Awareness of our identity choices is as important for how others perceive us as it is for our own decisions.

CHOOSING YOUR POINTS ON THE IDENTITY SEESAW

Identity is about belonging. We all belong to multiple groups in our families, our communities, and our societies. Within the academic space, most leaders belong to, and therefore identify with, multiple subcultures.

In my university, I belong to the communities of women faculty, social scientists, full professors, and globalists. As a former dean, I also identify with the university's senior leadership. One colleague's identity groups include faculty-of-color, pre-tenure assistant professors, and natural scientists. Another identifies with the Faculty Senate, non-tenure-track lecturers, humanities scholars, and postmodern theorists.

A good starting point is to examine some deep-seated truths about your place in the academy. Ask yourself, *Why am I in academia? In which part of my role do I feel happiest? Most competent? What does "faculty member" mean to me? What does "leader" or "administrator" mean to me? Do notions of "faculty," "leader," or "administrator" carry any loaded connotations for me?*

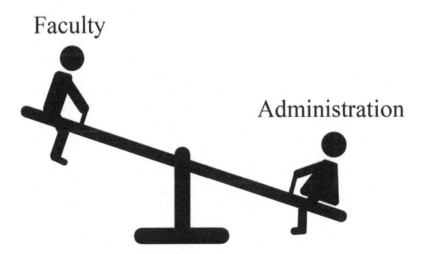

Figure 2.1. What Is My Professional Identity?

After you have asked yourself these questions, put similar ones to your most trusted confidantes. *What do you see as my primary professional identity? Whom do I tend to side with in controversial discussions? Do I exhibit any preference between faculty and administration? Do you perceive me as siding with one group over another?*

Consider what your and others' answers mean to you and how they influence your thinking, your behaviors, and your decisions. The answers may reveal that your "natural" position on the identity seesaw tilts heavily to one side or the other. There is nothing good or bad about where you naturally fall on the seesaw, so waste no time stressing about your identity. Each of us comes to our identity through a complex history that merits study, not criticism.

Rather, use the seesaw to identify where you need to grow. If you tend heavily toward one end, you will need to work to develop your less-natural identity to enhance your ability to engage effectively in all situations and with all constituencies.

From there, ask yourself where your identity lies on specific issues and controversies. For example, you may be engaged in conversations about faculty workload and the respective shares that teaching, scholarship, and service hold in your department's workload policy. What identities does such a conversation reveal in you? A department chair whose primary identity is as a teacher will approach such a discussion very differently from one whose primary identity is as a researcher.

Similarly, an administrative-identity leader will prioritize cost efficiencies in a workload discussion. She will maximize student-credit-hour production and research grant awards. A faculty-identity leader, in contrast, will look first to supporting faculty in their teacher-scholar roles, maximizing time for research while also attending to the department's classroom needs.

Neither of these is right or wrong. A good leader keeps her eye on the department's fiscal health *and* its faculty-friendly environment. Awareness of where you fall on the identity seesaw—which approach you bring to the table—will guide you in striking the proper balance between sometimes-competing priorities.

Your faculty identity is appropriate, and indeed essential, in critical areas of academic leadership. Faculty rightly want leaders who understand their point of view, unique experiences, and priorities. You will gain their trust and appreciation by exhibiting your faculty identity around key areas that are unique to the faculty experience.

Examples include issues related to academic freedom, promotion and tenure, research support, and pedagogy. Faculty's professional lives revolve around these topics, so approaching them wearing your purely "administrative" hat is likely to backfire. Rather, when engaging these issues, draw on your own faculty experience. State and repeat your deep understanding of how central these topics are to faculty experience and priorities. Lead with your faculty identity at the forefront.

An administrative identity, on the other hand, is increasingly important, especially for department chairs who often eschew this approach. In this era of budget cuts, declining enrollments, and soaring costs, no academic leader has the luxury of avoiding hard trade-offs. That means money—for programs, salaries, professional development, equipment, and more. An administrative frame of mind is essential when making budgetary decisions.

Strategic planning and thinking is another administratively oriented trait that all leaders must demonstrate. Because the highered landscape is changing so rapidly, leaders cannot continue with the way things have always been done.

You may have spent twenty years in a department operating under essentially the same curriculum, teaching methods, funding protocols, and assumptions about student expectations. Now you find yourself department chair, and the dean expects you to examine online courses, competency-based curricula, and your program's "workplace applicability." These types of upheavals make strategic planning and thinking—the prototypical administrator's activity—an essential skillset for academic leaders at all levels.

The identity seesaw will help you be thoughtful about your leadership choices as you face the variety of issues, challenges, and opportunities greeting you each day as an academic leader. It is important to stress that *you* must decide the identity balance that most works for you. Each leader's personal and professional history formulates a unique professional-identity profile. Similarly, each academic leader operates in a unique institutional context. The most important advice is that you be *aware* of your identity choices and deliberate in calibrating them to the situation you face.

ESSENTIAL IDEAS IN THIS CHAPTER

- Your professional identity greatly influences how you behave, make decisions, and are perceived by others.
- Most academic leaders emerge from the faculty ranks and thus feel a strong faculty identity.

- Newly appointed department chairs and deans frequently experience pressure to stay true to a faculty identity and not to adopt a leadership or administrative identity.
- Building a leadership identity is important to effective leadership.
- Academic leaders must strike a balance between faculty and administrative identities if they are to be effective bridges between the two constituencies.

THREE

Professional Role, or "Whose Team Are You On?"

Professional role is closely related to professional identity, but with some important distinctions. Whereas identity answers "where do I belong?" and "how do I define myself?" professional role asks "how do I behave?" and "whose interests do I represent?" Leaders frequently feel torn between playing for the "administrative" and "faculty" teams.

Until recently, college and university cultures promoted and accepted that department and program heads acted primarily as advocates for their own units and faculty. Even deans assumed the role of chief promoter of their school or college, leaving the strategic decision-making largely to the vice president for academic affairs, president, and board of trustees. At the department and school levels, the "leader-as-faculty-advocate" went largely unquestioned.

The great recession of 2008 and the decline in college enrollments that emerged in the years since have brought a sea change to the culture of leadership in American higher education. Newly appointed academic leaders feel a new pressure to identify as *institutional leaders*, not just as unit leaders.

This becomes truer each day as the assumptions on which colleges and universities operated for decades no longer apply. Institutions rely more than ever on leaders at all levels to think creatively, adopt new practices, and lead change. Presidents and provosts look to their deans, who in turn look to their department chairs and program directors, to combine the "faculty-advocate" role with the

25

"university leader" role. This is not because the senior leaders do not value faculty interests, but rather because the "chair-as-faculty-advocate" model no longer succeeds in meeting all the institution's objectives.

This shift in leadership expectations represents change that faculty sometimes resist. The us-versus-them culture makes new directors, chairs, and deans feel they have to decide whether they are playing for the faculty's or the administration's team. This "force to choose" is misguided in at least two important ways.

First, faculty and administrators alike play for the university's team, of course. All should be invested in seeing the institution thrive. Second, administrator and faculty interests intersect much more than they diverge. Financial health, student success, research productivity, a beautiful and well-functioning campus, a strong reputation—faculty and administrators alike enjoy the benefits of all of these and much more.

It is nonetheless important to recognize that faculty and administration sometimes have conflicting priorities. These typically revolve around resource distribution, faculty workload, and strategic direction. Faculty understandably prioritize faculty compensation and generous research support. In short, they commonly advocate for higher salaries and lighter course loads.

Administrators, acting as budgetary stewards, often find themselves on the opposing side in these conversations. Because personnel costs typically account for 85% or more of an institution's budget, increases in compensation packages carry enormous fiscal consequences. Similarly, the most important indicator of resource use is the student credit hour, as it is directly tied to tuition dollars. Administrators therefore have an incentive to dedicate their most expensive resource (faculty) to that activity that generates tuition (teaching).

Faculty and administration can also disagree on each other's role in decision-making, especially about major issues. Although most colleges and universities have explicit and detailed handbooks laying out roles and responsibilities around shared governance, disputes over decision-making authority remain common.

Faculty often argue they deserve a greater role in major decisions, including the university's strategic direction, major capital projects, and even sports programming. And while institutions' administration and boards of trustees typically have final say in determining the academic programs a school offers, faculty unsurprisingly contend that the curriculum lies firmly in their domain.

These differences arise from faculty's and administrators' distinct *role* in the university, not because either lacks an appreciation of the other's priorities. In the heat of debate, of course, it sometimes feels as if the two groups are playing on opposing teams. In those cases, both sides may ask their department heads and deans: "Whose team are you on?" The answer is that you are on the *institution's* team, but that you care about the perspectives and interests of both faculty and administration.

Effective leadership requires you to move back and forth along the faculty-administration seesaw as you carry out your role in pursuit of the institution's best interests. Deans, department chairs, and program directors share the unenviable, but absolutely critical, role of representing *both* the faculty's and administration's perspective to each other.

CHOOSING YOUR POINTS ON THE SEESAW

Your place on the advocate–team player seesaw is connected to your identity seesaw. The important difference is that the identity seesaw is about your projections of how you feel. The team seesaw is about your professional obligations, your role, and your responsibility. Your choices on this seesaw are revealed in your decisions and policies.

As you navigate the sometimes-treacherous landscape of faculty-administration politics, continue to assess your role and behaviors. Questions that can help in this self-reflection include, *Do I feel pressure to be loyal to either faculty or administration? Is this a case in which I have to choose a side? Do I fundamentally disagree with either the faculty or administration in this case? Do I detect an important imbalance of power in the discussion or decision-making? How can I reinforce that we're all on the same team?* As always, once you have asked yourselves these questions, put them to trusted and honest confidantes as well.

As argued above, the notion that leaders play for any one team enjoys elements of both myth and truth. The myth is that academic leaders must choose between working for the faculty or the administration. The truth is that they all play for the institution's team. This truth is a good starting place for determining your balance on the team seesaw.

Most leaders benefit from maximizing their time and orientation in the middle areas of this seesaw. Refuse to take sides (or appear to

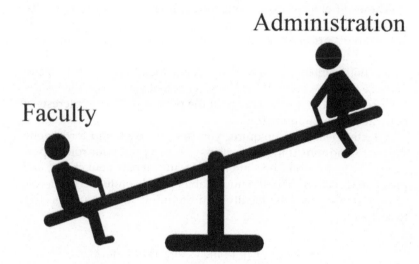

Figure 3.1. Whose Team Do I Play On?

do so), and instead frame issues as win-win. Push back against faculty and senior administrators urging you to occupy one end of the seesaw over the other. Instead, speak abundantly about commonly shared interests and your approach's benefits to all.

For example, many directors, chairs, and deans are currently engaged in curricular reform, both for their units' programs and for the institution's general-education curriculum. Decision-making around curricular reform frequently becomes controversial and framed in a "faculty-versus-administration" way.

Faculty play the defender of disciplinary standards, and the administration advocates for greater attention to experiential opportunities and skill-building. But curricular reform is not a battle that one side can win. Shared governance and students' needs necessitate that all members of the college community participate in both the process and implementation of launching a new curriculum.

If you choose one or the other of the seesaw's extremes in this case, you will alienate some of the partners you need on board. Placing yourself in the middle of the seesaw can help you diffuse the tension in this curricular debate and move toward a resolution.

By situating your role as an advocate for neither faculty nor administration, you can remind participants that *student* interests are paramount in this discussion and that reasonable compromises between disciplinary standards and professional readiness are available. Indeed, the two are not incompatible. Furthermore, you can illuminate the many common interests that all members of the university community have in revising curricula, including academic excellence, student success in the job market, and student demand for the institution's programs, among many others.

There are some instances in which it is appropriate to play for one team versus the other, but you should keep them to a minimum. First, when you genuinely and thoughtfully disagree with the position taken by either the faculty or the administration, your integrity demands that you say so. Sometimes you will do so in the closed sessions in which important decisions are debated. In other cases, you will do so in public. When you do, ensure that you explain that your reasoning is born not out of loyalty to one side or the other, but rather out of a desire to work in the institution's best interests.

A second situation that may lead you to choose a particular team is when you perceive a severe power imbalance. Colleges and universities have hierarchies, of course; power is not evenly distributed. But higher education is unique among American institutions in embracing shared governance, the notion that faculty join the administration in debating, formulating, and implementing the most important decisions and policies affecting the organization.

As "middle managers," directors, chairs, and deans have a special place to witness the power dynamics at work within shared governance. They can point out when one side—faculty or administration—presumes too much authority, failed to listen fully, or moved forward with a decision before full discussion has occurred. In this case, the academic leader rightly advocates for the inclusion of the excluded side's point of view.

On the few and carefully selected occasions in which you do choose one end of the seesaw over the other, do so explicitly. Use phrases such as "I'm going to advocate for the faculty here," or "I'm putting on my administrator hat now because I feel the leadership's point of view is getting lost," or "I've listened carefully to what you've presented. I disagree for the following reasons." This type of language suggests that you are motivated not by fealty to a side but rather to fairness and to reason.

Develop a reputation for spending the bulk of your time and approach in the middle of the team seesaw. It will help you build a reputation as an honest broker willing to listen to all constituencies. It will also model the important behavior of one who rejects the us-versus-them paradigm. Choose your decisions to take sides carefully and selectively. By doing so, you will add to your reputation as a person of integrity willing to disagree with both the senior leadership and the faculty.

ESSENTIAL IDEAS IN THIS CHAPTER

- The realities and challenges of the modern university have made the "chair-as-faculty-advocate" essentially obsolete.
- Academic leaders must balance their roles as advocates with those as team player for the entire institution.
- The "us-versus-them" culture that characterizes many institutions' faculty-administrative relations is largely unnecessary and undermines effective governance.
- Academic leaders should resist the "us-versus-them" framework and instead promote the intersection of faculty and administrative interests, as well as the health of the entire college or university.

FOUR

Leadership Comfort Zone

There was a time when program directors and department chairs could perform their jobs well by focusing on the day-to-day running of the department: leading faculty meetings, completing paperwork, writing evaluations, and smoothing out disputes among faculty. Their interactions with deans, provosts, and presidents were principally opportunities for them to promote their own department's interests and successes. Attention to detail and deadlines was as important a qualification as any other.

In today's higher-ed landscape, academic leaders, including at the department and program level, are called on to add *strategic planning and visionary leadership* to their skillset. Because academic programs are experiencing such upheaval—from budget shortfalls to declining enrollments to threatened program closure—each department and school head must be able both to manage daily operations and drive change in a strategic way.

The leadership comfort-zone seesaw asks you to consider where you feel most comfortable and competent in your role as academic leader: engaged in the details of the day-to-day operations or in envisioning the long-term success strategy for your unit? In what type of work do you engage easily and feel confident that you can do a good job? Conversely, in what areas do you feel less secure about your abilities, and find the work less enjoyable?

Detail-oriented leaders reliably complete tasks on time. They manage their email, paperwork, meetings, and other tasks with precision and by the deadline. They receive praise for "running a tight ship" and rarely get calls from the dean or provost asking about work that is late or shoddy.

Visionary leaders gain a reputation for asking big questions and for keeping their eye on long-term goals. They thrive in leading conversations about the unit's and the university's future. They are never criticized for failing to see the forest for the trees.

Few leaders excel on both ends of this seesaw, nor should they be expected to. Steve Jobs, founder and twice CEO of Apple, was one of the rare leaders who built a reputation as both a visionary and a details man. He foresaw a world full of personal computers *and* engaged personally (even obsessively) on every aspect of Apple product design.[1]

Jobs was also notoriously impossible to work for, micromanaging the brilliant people who worked for him and berating them when they failed to live up to his expectations. So perhaps his is not an example to follow.

Most of us tend toward one end of the seesaw. More than ever, we need to engage in both. Embracing leadership means dedicating time to ensuring that all the paperwork is in on time *and* that your unit will be thriving in five and ten years from now. This does not require becoming a Steve Jobs. Rather, it demands that you pay attention to and develop the leadership skills that fall outside your comfort zone.

CHOOSING YOUR POINTS ON THE SEESAW

The starting point for using the leadership comfort-zone seesaw is to honestly self-examine your talents and preferences. Assess your time allocation, as it is typically a strong indicator of your comfort zone. Spend two weeks tracking your tasks and activities. Do you spend the bulk of your time keeping the operation running? Or on long-term thinking, building relationships, and designing initiatives? What types of tasks do you complete on time? Which lead you to procrastinate? These questions are for information-gathering purposes, not judgment. There is no shame in preferring daily operations to strategic planning. Rather, it is the first step to knowing those areas in which you must grow your skillset.

Once you have a clear picture of your own self-assessment, ask others about your strengths and preferences. Ask open ended questions like "Which parts of my job do I do well?" and "I want to be a more effective leader—what do you think I should work on?" Then

Detail-oriented

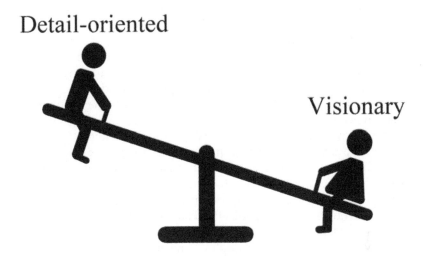

Visionary

Figure 4.1.   Where Is My Leadership Comfort Zone?

sit back and listen with all the non-defensiveness you can muster. You need not accept all the information you receive, but you will undoubtedly gain perspectives on your performance that are different from your own.

Being open to second and third opinions is important, as our capacity for misunderstanding ourselves is high. A frequent blind spot comes from our tendency to downplay the importance of those tasks we find less satisfying.

The individual who rarely seems to deliver paperwork on time argues that deadlines are "arbitrary." The program director whose self-study is rushed and lacking in vision claims that program review is a waste of time. Asking for, and accepting, others' observations on your tendencies is a critical resource for finding your blind spots about your own strengths and weaknesses.

A common complaint among academic leaders is that they are so burdened by day-to-day demands that they have little or no time for long-term planning. Where this is genuinely true, individuals should address it. Ask for more help, delegate better, and train your staff to develop new proficiencies.

More often, however, academic leaders allow themselves to get overwhelmed. Perhaps counterintuitively, this happens to both detail-oriented and visionary leaders. The former's comfort zone is in the details, so he spends most of his time there. He also hates to leave any task unfinished or not meeting his exacting standards. He fills all of his professional time on the details and still feels dissatisfied and overwhelmed.

The visionary leader is sometimes a poor time and resource manager. Because she pays little attention to the details, the paperwork, deadlines, and day-to-day duties pile up. Under pressure to deliver on these, she becomes overwhelmed with the volume of tasks in need of completion.

This is why genuine self-examination of your habits, strengths, and weaknesses is so valuable. It helps you not only identify your preferences but also address the pitfalls that your preference carries. To be sure, the day-to-day work of running a unit is time-consuming, but productive leaders manage it well. Strategic and visionary work *do* require more planning ahead and formal allocations of time and effort. Department retreats, do-not-disturb hours, and dedicated strategic meetings are examples of means to carve out time for this important work.

Determining where to place yourself on the leadership comfort-zone seesaw is fairly straightforward. Most tasks are readily located on the scale. Exercises such as strategic planning, major curricular reform, and engaging your department in academic-program-review activity lie at the visionary end of the continuum. Completing paperwork, attending meetings, and managing students' myriad issues lie on the day-to-day end of the spectrum.

There are tasks that fall in the center and require you to draw on elements from both visionary and detailed skillsets. Some tasks appear detail-oriented but benefit from some strategic thinking. Learning-outcomes assessment and annual performance evaluations, for instance, can feel like deadline-oriented tasks that just need to get done. Both, however, benefit from your keeping strategic goals in mind when completing them.

The course schedule is another task that benefits from a center-balance on the leadership comfort-zone seesaw. Too many chairs and directors view the course schedule as a perfunctory and bothersome task: collect the faculty's preferences and fit them into the classrooms and time blocks as best you can. That approach misses an opportunity to use the course schedule strategically in a way that enhances student success, increases graduation rates, and maximizes faculty resources.

A strategic approach to the course schedule begins by developing goals for the exercise—for example, maximize course availability for students, efficient use of classroom space, spread curriculum out across all five weekdays, and place the most effective teachers in first-year courses. The schedule is then built to meet as many of these goals as possible, with faculty preferences for particular days and times one of many competing priorities.

This type of exercise draws on a leader's ability to bring together the faculty to discuss and agree to common goals, and to sacrifice their individual preferences to students' best interests. Leading such an effort is challenging, for sure, but can yield enormous results around student success. And it calls on a skillset that is hugely different from that required to build a spreadsheet of classrooms, time blocks, and courses.

Another example of a task falling in the middle of this seesaw is running faculty meetings. Faced with a full agenda and an hour time block, you might feel that getting through all the items requires you to focus on your "detail" skills. Indeed, running an efficient meeting in which tangents and tirades are kept at a minimum is an essential "detail" skills.

Nonetheless, every occasion to gather your faculty together avails you of a crucial opportunity advance the unit's visionary and strategic goals. Remind participants of how the agenda items relate to the unit's long-term objectives. Manage disruptors and tangent-talkers by refusing to allow them to divert the meeting's focus. Challenge the group to discuss issues within the framework of the department's and the college's strategic plans. By framing detailed items within contexts that promote a long-term vision, you not only keep the trains running on time but also reinforce the importance of the destination.

The nature of your academic leadership position requires that you draw on skills across the full spectrum of the leadership comfort-zone seesaw. The keys to success are knowing your preferences, building your skills in your out-of-comfort area, and thinking carefully about where on the seesaw you should situate yourself for the issue at hand.

ESSENTIAL IDEAS IN THIS CHAPTER

- Most leaders tend toward strength in either strategic thinking or detailed implementation.
- You should exploit your strengths in the leadership comfort zone and build skills in the area that comes less naturally to you.

- Some tasks that appear to be simply about implementation actually benefit from strategic thinking and design. The course schedule is an important example.
- Strategic thinking and planning are often set aside as academic leaders are mired in the abundant tasks of getting the day-to-day job done. If this is your situation, carve out time for strategic activities.

NOTE

1. Joe Nocera, "What Makes Steve Jobs Great?" *New York Times*, August 26, 2011.

FIVE

Decision-Making Style

An abundant literature on decision-making in the business world instructs leaders on how to make the best decisions for their organizations.[1] It is noteworthy that so many academics working in schools of business examine decision-making in corporate environments, but fail to apply their work to nonprofits and to higher education especially. An important exception is Jim Collins, author of the highly influential *Good to Great*,[2] who wrote a companion monograph specifically aimed at what he labeled "social sectors," educational institutions included.[3]

Decision-making in higher education has received some attention, though typically not from business-school researchers. Academic and educator William Coscarelli, for example, generated an inventory to help leaders identify their decision-making style in educational settings.[4] Garland highlights the effect of academic culture on academic decision-makers in times of great change.[5] Under the auspices of the American Council on Education, Peter Eckel has written presciently about the decision-making challenges leaders face in today's higher-ed environment characterized by declining enrollments, increasing costs, and reductions in public financing.[6]

Decision-making in academia differs from that in the corporate world in at least two important ways. First, most academic departments are run on tradition and consensus, rather than on strict hierarchies and explicit rules. Second, shared governance means that faculty expect to be consulted on, and even to decide on, many of the major decisions made within an academic unit and even the institution as a whole.

"Transparency" has emerged as the word to capture the faculty's desire for consultation and inclusion in decision-making. A few areas fall clearly within the realm of "shared" between faculty and administration—academic program development is the most obvious. Most, however, fall into a gray area where the boundaries of decision-making authority are not clearly demarcated.

Within individual departments or schools, that lack of clarity often magnifies. Faculty understandably seek out greater authority closer to home, that is, in their departments and schools. At the same time, departments and schools often have *less-well*-articulated rules around decision-making than the university does. This means that chairs and deans face greater pressure to be inclusive even while they have fewer rules that define to what extent they must consult faculty on any given issue.

This dynamic puts academic leaders in a frustrating position. They meet the dual pressures of "transparency" and "efficiency" in how they approach decisions. The decision-making seesaw can help.

For our purposes, the decision-making dimensions academic leaders need to consider are those on the centralized-democratic continuum. A centralized model puts decision-making in the hands of the director, chair, or dean. A democratic model places responsibility for decision-making in the hands of the unit's faculty, which may draw on formal or informal methods to arrive at a decision.

Few, if any, academic units employ either extreme on the decision-making seesaw. No chair has complete authority over decisions in her department, and no dean puts every decision to a faculty vote. Nonetheless, some units, especially academic departments, develop strong cultures around one side or the other of the decision-making seesaw.

In centralized departments, the chair enjoys the authority to make decisions about everything that isn't explicitly reserved for department input and votes, typically the curriculum, hiring, and promotion and tenure decisions. In such departments, faculty value the time they save because the chair is empowered to make decisions on everything from the course schedule to committee assignments to student award recipients. This model moves into the danger zone when a director or chair becomes all-powerful, making unilateral decisions and neglecting faculty voices in the major issues that affect the department's future.

In democratic departments, the chair acts as a convener, creating the forums for faculty feedback and implementing the will of the majority. Department faculty meet frequently to discuss and decide on issues. Votes are taken on everything ranging from who will represent the department at university events to the course schedule to planning the family reception at the end of the year. The extreme, and unhealthy, versions of this model include departments that hold discussions and votes around items such as the menu at the office picnic, the type font on student certificates, and the credit approval for a student's study-abroad course.

Neither decision-making model is *a priori* best. So long as they are practiced within healthy limits, both democratic and centralized departments and schools can achieve high productivity and faculty satisfaction. Rather, a unit's decision-making approach should be fine-tuned to the tasks it needs to achieve and to the people who work in it.

Too often, departments and schools rely on decision-making cultures that made sense for one era but are ill-equipped to manage today's challenges, tasks, and expectations. In many cases, academic units evolved to employ an informal, consensus-based decision-making system. The department head would check in with faculty—either informally or through meetings—before making most decisions. Faculty meetings might be spent on lengthy conversations about a variety of issues, most of which did not involve the types of existential questions that many programs face today.

What has changed? First, demands on faculty are greater than ever before. Research expectations have increased at nearly all colleges and universities in the last fifty years, meaning faculty must devote more time to scholarly pursuits. This coincides with a greater (and much-needed) focus on "student success," which requires faculty to become ever more proficient in teaching and advising.

Add to this mix the demands of program and learning-outcomes assessment. Assessment activities consume large chunks of time, both in the planning on how to carry them out and in their implementation. These are just three of the most important changes in workload and performance expected of the faculty member in 2020.

To these increasingly time-consuming activities are added the need for departments to make weighty and often revolutionary changes. As recently as fifteen years ago, many departments and schools were not expected to create strategic plans or engage in demand analyses for their program offerings. When faculty retired or left the university, they were regularly replaced, usually with little change in how their position was defined. Deans and department heads were rarely faced with dramatic cuts to their budgets, and prospective students asked few questions about employability and salary expectations associated with individual programs.

Decision-making cultures at the department and school level have not adapted to these changes in faculty life. Many department cultures remain on the time-consuming "democratic" end of the seesaw. Furthermore, as described in chapter 2, department heads and program directors are increasingly expected to behave as *leaders*, not just as conveners or task managers. This suggests that many units could benefit from moving eastward on the seesaw, delegating small and medium-level decisions to the department head, and leaving democratic procedures for the truly strategic decisions affecting the department.

CHOOSING YOUR POINTS ON THE SEESAW

Finding the right point on the decision-making seesaw is perhaps the most fraught of all the balancing acts presented in this book. This is because two forces, working at odds to one another, are operating in higher education today.

The first, discussed at length in chapters 2 and 3, is the need for department heads and deans to balance advocacy for their units with university-wide priorities. This means you must inject strategic thinking and goal-oriented planning into nearly all your unit's activities and decisions. This effect nudges you toward the centralized side of the seesaw, not because you are undemocratic, but because yours is the voice reminding the group of long-term goals, strategic objectives, and budget realities.

The second, and opposite, force is faculty's reassertion of their role in shared governance. Across the United States, faculty unions, councils, assemblies, and other representative bodies are rising up against what they see as administrators making major decisions with too little faculty input. In severe cases, this trend manifests in votes of no confidence and even resignations of presidents, provosts, and deans. More often, it leads to faculty feeling, and voicing, dissatisfaction and general disappointment both about decisions taken by the administration and with the reduced authority faculty enjoy. In such cases, both faculty morale and trust in leaders are low.

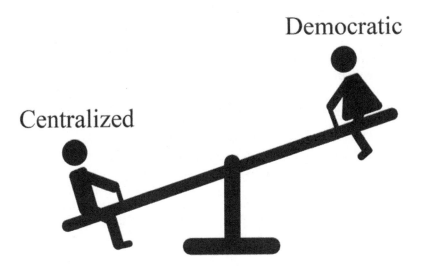

Figure 5.1.   What Is My Decision-Making Style?

This countereffect's impact on department heads and deans is to nudge them to the democratic end of the decision-making seesaw. If you perceive your faculty are frustrated with lack of transparency and inclusion at the president and provost levels, your natural tendency is to err on the democratic side of the seesaw in your own management of your unit. When faced with a faculty unhappy about perceived exclusion, you will make every effort to be inclusive.

This tension between centralized and democratic decision-making brings home how difficult striking the right decision-making balance is for today's academic leaders. You will feel strong pressures pulling you in both directions. How then to know where to situate yourself on the decision-making seesaw for the many situations, challenges, and issues you face?

You should consider two aspects of the decision-making seesaw. First is the unit's decision-making culture and traditions. Where do they fall on the centralized-democratic balance?

Second, ask yourself what balance *you* prefer as the unit's chief decision-maker. At what level of decision-making authority and autonomy do you feel comfortable? How does that interact with the department's expectations and the genuine need for inclusion? Map each of these and examine any gaps between your preferred decision-making style and the department's culture.

Once you have defined both the department culture and your own preferences, ask, "Is this decision-making culture working for our unit?" Evidence to answer this question lies in how well decisions are received and in how long they endure.

Robust decisions enjoy the acceptance of nearly all members of the faculty, including those who opposed them. They emerge from a process that is well understood and embraced by the group. Even when a decision goes against an individual's preference, she accepts the decision's legitimacy. These decisions go on to implementation and typically enjoy a long life in practice.

In contrast, an unhealthy decision-making culture reveals itself in decisions that are continually contested after they are made. Faculty seek to revisit the decision and may even undermine its implementation. They complain that the decision-making process was unfair, non-transparent, or non-inclusive. The turmoil surrounding decisions divides the department and undermines the chair's ability to lead it to a successful future. These decisions often go unheeded and require revision in short order.

In most cases, it will be fairly clear which issues require full faculty input and even vote. Curriculum, hiring, and promotion and tenure have already been mentioned. In some instances, particularly in small departments, committee assignments, academic advisor assignments, and academic program review authorship will also fall on the full-inclusion end of the seesaw.

Similarly, many of the mundane decisions a chair makes throughout the day fall clearly in the head's office: course substitutions, catalog edits, responses to the dean or provost, delegation of work to the administrative assistant, scheduling of faculty meetings.

The types of decisions that fall in between are the challenge. You must balance decision-making efficiency with the needs and desires for faculty to be included. The course schedule is a particularly thorny one for many units. Some department faculty sit in a room each semester and collectively create next semester's schedule. In others, the chair makes the schedule and delivers it to the faculty. In most, faculty input is delivered through their submission of their preferred schedule, which the chair promises to take into account in finalizing the course schedule.

As is discussed in the previous chapter, however, the course schedule is much more than an exercise in maximizing faculty preferences. It is, rather, one of the most important tools we have to maximize student success. So when you examine your decision-making options around the course schedule, be sure to include student success in your calculations.

This might represent a culture change that necessitates a middle-of-the-seesaw approach. You as the leader may present the decision to move toward a student-oriented scheduling model (centralized), but you should include faculty discussion about the implementation of the new practice (democratic).

Curriculum is another middle-of-the-seesaw topic. In many academic programs, curriculum falls fully on the democratic end of the balance. Faculty committees propose curricular content, and the department votes on it. Again, in today's changing higher-ed landscape, academic leaders usually have to insert themselves into curricular discussions in ways they did not before.

As discussed in chapter 3, faculty and administration sometimes argue over who has authority in designing and approving curriculum. At the department level, especially, the decision-making seesaw can help a chair or director navigate these turbulent waters. You might be tempted to leave curricular content fully to the faculty committee to propose and to the faculty body to approve. Such a democratic approach would no doubt prove the path of least resistance, but it could put your program at risk.

In designing program curricular requirements, faculty typically look to their disciplinary histories and standards, their own educational backgrounds, and their sense of disciplinary excellence. Increasingly, these priorities clash with student interests in programs focused on work skills, fast and lucrative employment opportunities, and professional degrees.

All evidence points to the decline in students seeking out a college degree for the experience of learning and the concomitant rise in students seeking professional skills that will immediately serve them in the workplace. Deep disciplinary expertise is losing ground to skills-based learning among college-bound students.

This rift between what faculty and students prioritize in developing academic programs plays out in contentious debates in colleges and universities across the country. The arguments are not between faculty and students, but between faculty who value their disciplinary proficiency and administrators who follow student preferences and enrollment trends. Neither group is wrong; they simply bring different perspectives and priorities to the discussion.

How does this influence the academic leader's choice on the decision-making seesaw? It means that leaving curriculum only to the faculty (its historic position) runs the risk of developing programs that are out of step with student demand. The effective leader instead locates himself somewhere to the left of full democracy on the seesaw, a place that respects the strong faculty role in curriculum but also assures that the reality in student preferences is reflected in the outcome.

The decision-making seesaw requires you to constantly rebalance. This is especially true in today's environment in which the sands are shifting below us on everything from shared governance to how we define our institutional missions. On any given day, your approach may well be on locations all across its spectrum.

You should centralize sufficiently to complete the unit's work and to assure that decisions serve the unit's and the institution's strategic goals. You should democratize sufficiently to ensure decisions that are both enduring and embraced. Regular attention to the decision-making seesaw's dynamics will help you pitch your approach successfully.

ESSENTIAL IDEAS IN THIS CHAPTER

- Academic leaders should draw on decision-making approaches ranging from centralized to democratic according to the problem at hand.
- Absence of a mutually understood division of authority between faculty and administration in institutions' shared governance complicates academic leaders' decision-making environments.
- Departments that lean too heavily on either democratic or centralized decision-making practices run the risk of inefficient and poor decisions.
- Many academic units rely on long-standing decision-making cultures that no longer fit the unit's needs and realities.
- A healthy decision-making balance is revealed by decisions that enjoy legitimacy and strong implementation.

NOTES

1. Tim Brown, *Change by Design* (New York: Harperbusiness, 2009); Daniel Kahneman, Dan Lovallo, and Olivier Sibony, eds., *HBR's 10 Must Reads on Making Smart Decisions* (Cambridge: Harvard Business Review Press, 2013).

2. Jim Collins, *Good to Great: Why Some Companies Make the Leap and Others Don't* (New York: Harper, 2001).

3. Jim Collins, *Good to Great for the Social Sectors: Why Business Thinking is Not the Answer* (New York: Harper, 2005).

4. William C. Coscarelli, *Decision-Making Style Inventory*, 1st ed. (San Francisco: John Wiley and Sons, 2007).

5. James Garland, *Saving Alma Mater: A Rescue Plan for America's Public Universities* (Chicago: University of Chicago Press, 2009).

6. Peter D. Eckel, *The Shifting Frontiers of Academic Decision Making: Responding to New Priorities, Following New Pathways*, ACE/Praeger Series on Higher Education (Lanham, MD: Rowman and Littlefield, 2006).

SIX

Management Style

friendly boss

Leadership development literature coming out of the business sphere is replete with discussions comparing leaders and managers.[1] Typically in these conversations, managers emerge as the less impressive and less impactful of the two. Leaders transform organizations, it is said, while managers merely organize people and their activities. Any implied disparagement of managers is unfortunate, as it is the rare individual who has the skills to *manage*, that is, to supervise a team of diverse individuals and to coordinate their work effectively.

Academic leaders *are* managers. That is, they supervise, direct, coordinate, and evaluate those who report to them. Some are chairs of small departments, supervising three or four faculty and a shared administrative assistant. Others are deans of massive schools, overseeing a complex web of assistant deans, department chairs, program directors, diverse professional staff, and a large faculty. In both cases, and in every instance in between, academic leaders must perform the delicate task of managing a group of independently minded people (faculty) in a setting characterized by the absence of strict hierarchies.

The management-style seesaw asks how you approach your relationship to those you supervise. Do you situate yourself as the boss, a colleague, or even a friend? The fact that department chairs and deans come from faculty ranks and typically return to faculty generates special challenges.

To be both an equal within the group but also the leader responsible for decisions is a tricky balancing act. You are at once colleague and supervisor of those you serve and lead. The management-style seesaw contrasts a "boss" approach with that of a
"friend/colleague."

Department chairs and program directors frequently bemoan
their lack of authority, owing it to the fact that they will return to
the faculty they now lead. A typical lament goes something like,
"How can I insist that Robert change his behavior? He will resent
me and take it out on me upon my return to faculty and when he
becomes chair."

Rarely do those leaders who voice this frustration closely examine the assumptions underlying their complaint. The first is that a
chair who exercises her authority to hold underperforming or badly
behaved faculty members will necessarily experience retribution
when that same faculty member later is appointed chair.

A second assumption is that faculty do not truly want a strong
leader, but rather a paper-pusher who will take care of the chair's
tasks and mostly leave them alone. It follows that a chair who exerts
her authority should expect a chilly reception upon returning to
faculty.

It is important to unpack these assumptions, especially because
they undermine the confidence of many who show high potential as
effective leaders. Both are grounded in the misbelief that department faculty will not *appreciate* the activist chair's initiatives and
interventions. Remember that managing a problem faculty member
improves the department climate overall, and usually the rest of the
faculty's morale. Rather than predict how people will react in the
culture that *currently* exists, expect their reaction *after* you have
meaningfully addressed problems and instituted needed change.
Overwhelmingly, faculty express gratitude for this type of leadership, even when the process was painful.

Let us first look at the "retribution" assumption, in which a department head resists exerting authority for fear of "payback" when
the object of his action later becomes head. Such an outcome is
possible, but less likely than most imagine. Faculty who are chronic
problems—either because of performance or (lack of) professional
behavior—rarely become department heads. Deans avoid problem
faculty as department leaders, as they are terrible role models and
frequently troublemakers. Nor do deans want to deal with difficult
personalities in their chairs' council.

Furthermore, the assumption that "they'll get their revenge on me later" forgets that the rest of the department likely abhors the individual's behavior and will support the chair in their intervention. The chair's intervention not only addresses the problem behavior but also often weakens the individual's standing in the department as well.

Even in departments in which faculty take turns as chair in a rotating system, the strong chair enjoys some protection. Any decent dean will be aware of and support a strong chair's necessary intervention with a difficult or underperforming faculty member. In appointing a new chair, even when it is the previously difficult faculty member herself, the dean will communicate his expectation that the problem behavior not reemerge. Similarly, most deans will go to great lengths not to appoint as chair the kind of individual who would engage in retribution over a colleague.

The second assumption, that department faculty prefer weak chairs who complete tedious tasks but do not assert real authority, also suffers under scrutiny. There is no doubt that faculty are peculiarly independent and resistant to being managed in their day-to-day activities. That said, faculty recognize problems and benefit when a strong department chair addresses them. If the chair exerts authority in a manner that effects meaningful and positive change, the vast majority of faculty will appreciate it, even if they express resistance in the moment of change.

Similarly, faculty suffer in departments that are dysfunctional or poorly managed. No one is happy in a department characterized by lack of student success, an outdated curriculum, poorly run faculty meetings, and bullies run amok. Such a culture begs for a chair willing to take authority seriously and to assert it with those resistant to change. Except for those faculty who are the source of the problems, your colleagues will thank you for it.

None of this is to say that the transition from faculty to department head or dean is easy, for the leader or for the former colleagues. It is to say, however, that many of would-be leaders' worst fears about how faculty will handle their newfound authority are unfounded.

A particularly tricky transition from colleague to supervisor comes when some of your faculty are close friends. The idea of supervising their friends terrifies many new chairs and directors. They cannot imagine writing friends' performance evaluations, much less intervening on a performance or behavioral issue. Yet thousands of academic leaders do just that each year, usually without the angst or conflict they imagine.

If you experience anxiety about the idea of supervising those faculty who are also your friends, the best option is to have a serious discussion before you assume the post. Begin by acknowledging that you value the relationship and look forward to its thriving into the future. Then discuss openly how some things will have to change given your professional transition into the leadership role.

Try something like this:

> Michael, you and I have been colleagues and friends. Both of those relationships are important to me. Now that I will be department chair, some things will change. I won't be able to engage in gossip about the department or the administration when our families have weekend get-togethers. You'll have to understand that I can't favor your requests for course blocks or graduate assignments. I'd like to ask you to respect these types of things and not put me in an awkward position that would lead me to behave unprofessionally or unfairly to others.

A true friend and a good colleague could not but agree with these reasonable requests. Your success as an academic leader and your professional integrity demand them. However, if your friends see you as an ally in the department's power politics or expect that you will share the dirt on what happens at dean's meetings, you will have to disappoint. Sometimes, friendships do not endure one friend's becoming program director, chair, or dean. But it is rare, and it typically suggests that one friend was making unreasonable expectations of the other.

Managing people is hard. This is especially true in the academy, where hierarchies are loose and faculty do not always recognize their leaders' power. The management-style seesaw can help you design your approach to each individual and situation. Some call for you to behave as a colleague, and even as a friend. Others will require a fairly heavy supervisor or boss hat. Most will draw on the spaces in between.

The space in the middle of this seesaw, that between "friend" and "boss," is especially interesting. Almost everyone would agree that they would like to work with a "friendly boss," but few would delight at working with a "bossy friend." The first connotes an individual confident in his authority who exercises it with kindness and compassion. The second suggests one whose primary role is as a friend, but who orders people around.

This distinction points to why it is important for you to talk with your friends about your role as leader. You *are* the boss and will have to act like one sometimes. Your true friends will recognize that, as a friendly boss, you will exercise your authority.

CHOOSING YOUR POINTS ON THE SEESAW

Eventually, all productive academic leaders find themselves on every point of the management-style seesaw. The vast array of tasks, situations, and people they manage each demand their own approach, drawn from the full spectrum of choices. Leaders who refuse to employ one or other of the seesaw's extremes—the dean who does not deign to treat faculty as colleagues, or the chair who proclaims she will never be "the boss"—rob themselves of important management tools.

Once you have embraced the understanding that you need to draw on all points of the management seesaw, consider your strengths and weaknesses in the management skillset. As with the other balancing acts introduced in this book, begin by reflecting on your preferences, comfort zone, and habits.

Questions to ask include: Which management mode do I express most frequently? Under stress? Does one end of the seesaw cause me more anxiety than the other? What types of issues and chal-

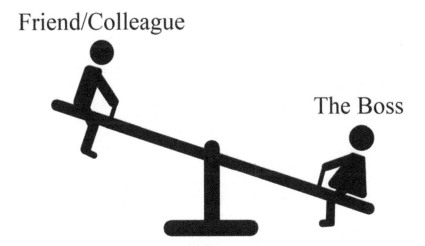

Figure 6.1. What Is My Management Style?

lenges bring each mode out in me? Do I tend to succeed better with one management strategy over another? As always, once you have asked yourself these questions, query others on similar themes, and listen carefully to their observations of your behavior.

Now aware of your own proclivities, approach each management scenario with careful thought about which colleague-boss balance best fits the moment. Doing so helps you to pitch your management in a way that works best for your faculty and staff and, therefore, increases your chances for success. That said, there are recurrent situations in academia that call for more of one management approach or the other.

Academic departments, programs, and even schools rarely operate on strict hierarchical terms in which a boss gives orders to subordinates and expects them to be carried out. Rather, faculty enjoy enormous autonomy in determining everything from the content of their courses and research to the amount of time they spend on campus. This atmosphere means that most of your daily interactions will lie on the "colleague" side of the seesaw.

Similarly, because most faculty *do* recognize that the chair must exercise supervisory oversight, they follow directions when offered in a collegial way. Most chairs can assign individuals to committees, develop the course schedule, urge volunteers for weekend events, and oversee important faculty meetings without having to draw heavily on their "boss" side of the spectrum. In healthy and high-functioning departments, the director-as-colleague predominates and succeeds.

There are also some issues tailor-made for a collegial approach. One is in your support and mentoring of junior faculty. The department head has the benefit of experience as a (former) junior faculty member and all the challenges it entails. Draw on that experience in an empathetic way as you provide advice for faculty in their pre-tenure years. Of course, you must add a dash of the supervisor in clearly articulating expectations and pointing out any shortcomings in the individual's performance. But the bulk of your engagement should be encouraging and supportive. Junior faculty experience sufficient pre-tenure stress. An aggressive department head who shows more stick than carrot need not be among them.

A second area that nearly always calls for the head to act as a colleague is in guiding department discussions that require the input of all faculty. Decisions that go to a vote—for example, new hires and promotion and tenure verdicts—are best formulated during a conversation among equals. In these cases, the department head keeps the discussion on track and perhaps reminds members of the strategic goals surrounding the issue at hand. But when it comes to engaging in the content of the decision, she acts as a colleague, listening well to others and sharing her opinion as any other member would.

The vast majority of department chairs and program directors, and even many deans, prefer the "colleague" approach in nearly all settings. It is nonetheless important for academic leaders to develop their "boss" skills and to selectively employ them when necessary.

One task that requires your supervisory skills is in evaluating faculty and staff. For many, this is the most detested part of the job. Your professional responsibility requires you to shed any favoritism or affection you have toward individuals and evaluate each one on agreed-on criteria. It also requires you to clearly articulate when an individual falls short of the expectations.

Many chairs find it especially difficult to put in writing that a faculty member is underperforming. Part of the culture guiding interactions among faculty is that we do not openly criticize each other. Doing so in a formal evaluation feels unkind to the faculty and deeply uncomfortable for the department head. But written evaluations are an essential part of a leader's duties and required for a well-functioning department. Faculty and staff cannot improve their performance if their leader has failed to clarify the expectations and problems.

The "boss" hat is also necessary when confronting difficult people and behaviors. Too many academic units suffer from years of unprofessional behavior and lackluster performance going unchecked because a succession of chairs, directors, and deans have failed to address such personnel problems.

Leaders who have a reputation for relying on the "friend" end of the management seesaw can, surprisingly, become both the least and most effective in asserting their "boss" skillset. In the first instance, the collegially-oriented department head who eschews the boss role does so because he is conflict avoidant or unskilled in managing faculty. Underperformers and difficult colleagues readily learn that the department head is unable to confront them and thus continue their problematic behaviors. Sadly, the high performers and good citizens will learn the same thing and likely become resentful.

In the second instance, the usually collegial leader instead becomes especially effective when selectively exercising her "boss" muscles. Accustomed to the head's typically generous demeanor, the problem faculty member wrongly presumes she is unwilling to confront and hold him accountable. So when the leader writes an honest evaluation and sets expectations for behavioral and performance improvements, the faculty member is stunned into paying attention. In this case, it is specifically because the "boss" behavior is so rare that the faculty member takes notice and is more likely to respond.

Playing the "boss" role does not imply that you are unkind or harsh. It simply means that you overtly exercise your authority as leader of the unit in the case at hand. You demonstrate your willingness to take your position seriously and to hold people responsible for performing their duties well and in a professional manner. You are also in your "boss" role when you celebrate faculty achievements and write glowing performance evaluations. In both critical and celebratory moments, you exercise the authority that comes with your title.

Academic workplaces are especially thorny places for leaders, especially those without training, to learn the hard work of personnel management. The management-style seesaw helps you develop approaches that range from playing the boss when you must to playing the colleague that you also are.

This seesaw can be particularly helpful at the beginning of your leadership term, when you establish relationships, expectations, and patterns of interaction with your faculty and staff. It is also a useful tool to return to time and again to examine and adjust your management approaches to the dizzying array of people, problems, and opportunities that arise in your daily life.

ESSENTIAL IDEAS IN THIS CHAPTER

- Academic leaders face an especially tricky balance between their roles as colleagues and that of the boss.
- Too many department chairs presume that they cannot assert authority among their colleagues because one day they will return to the faculty and receive retribution.
- Engage in explicit conversations with your colleagues and friends about the changing nature of your respective professional roles before you assume your leadership post.
- Effective leaders spend most of their management time in the "colleague" domain yet employ the "boss" role selectively and under necessary circumstances.

NOTE

1. John P. Kotter, "Management Is (Still) Not Leadership," *Harvard Business Review*, January 9, 2013; Vineet Nayar, "Three Differences between Managers and Leaders," *Harvard Business Review*, August 2, 2013.

SEVEN

Availability

Among the most common complaints that new directors, chairs, and deans report is that they have too little time to address the multitude of tasks facing them each day. The increased demands of the position eat up more work hours than they anticipated. More meetings, more paperwork, and more people voicing requests and complaints combine to mean more hours in the office and less time to dedicate to other pursuits, including teaching and research. For some, the burdens of task management lead not only to stress, but to unhappiness and even poor performance.

Time management is *essential* for an effective academic leader. Yet few give it much thought before or even during their terms in leadership. They instead rely on the same patterns and strategies to complete their leadership work as they did in their previous position, an approach that rarely succeeds. When your position and duties change, it follows that your time and task allocation must change as well.

This is not a chapter on time management per se, but rather on that subset of time management that relates to your *availability*. Your availability to all constituents—students, faculty, staff, senior administrators, parents, community members—must be managed wisely if you are to succeed in leadership and maintain a healthy work/life balance.

The availability seesaw has two components: on campus and electronic. One extreme for both on-campus and electronic availability is "round the clock." This individual is available for walk-in visits and by text and email essentially all the time. On the other extreme is "working hours and appointments only." A leader on this extreme of the seesaw insists on scheduled appointments during working hours for all professional interactions except true emergencies.

As an academic leader, you should develop an *availability strategy* that meets your dual goals of being accessible to your many constituents and also saving private time to work. This is important not only for your own efficiency but also to model best practices to others as well. Furthermore, your strategy must meet two criteria: that your colleagues be able to contact you easily, and that you respond to them within the timeframe necessary to address their concerns. Our discussion of the availability seesaw revolves around these goals.

MANAGING YOUR ON-CAMPUS AVAILABILITY

The Open Door

Most department chairs and program directors opt toward the "open door" end of the seesaw. They typically practiced a version of this strategy before they assumed the leadership post. In their new role, they seek to project that they are even *more* available than ever, so they enhance the open-door strategy to something close to "open door, all the time." Perhaps the previous head had a reputation for not being available, so they make an extra effort to make themselves easy to find.

The open-door extremist occupies his office Monday through Friday and keeps his door always open, except during private meetings and telephone calls with individuals. Furthermore, the open door indicates, "I'm available. Just walk in if you'd like to talk."

Certainly, this type of availability makes you visible and accessible. There are nonetheless some important problems with a rigorous open-door policy. The first is simply that it can eat up too much of your time. An open door that broadcasts, "I'm here if you want to chat," also suggests that your highest priority is to do just that.

As department head, you will discover more people seek to chat with you than before, typically because they either want something from you or they want you to hear their opinion. Neither of these is wrong, and indeed you are obliged to listen to both. But neither is urgent or necessarily the best use of your time in the moment.

Figure 7.1. How Do I Manage My On-Campus Availability?

A subset of this problem is that the open-door policy puts no limit on how long visitors can *remain*. Most understand you are busy and will not overstay their welcome. Many departments, however, have at least one faculty member who appears to have abundant time and willingness to chat with you, rarely giving thought to how the conversation may be robbing you of essential minutes to attend to your duties.

You are thus put in the awkward position of suggesting the person depart or enduring a growing frustration at the conversation's length. You put yourself at risk of becoming the cranky department head who resents how much time colleagues are taking but is unwilling to change availability practices for fear it will give a bad impression.

Another related issue concerns how academic leaders react to the downsides of the open-door policy. Upon finding that they cannot complete their duties while *in* the office, they retreat to places *outside* the office for peace and quiet. Of course, selective and limited blocks of time working from home or the coffee shop are an appropriate time-management strategy. But taken too far, it can reverse the effect the chair had hoped to create with an open-door policy: on-campus presence and availability.

Leaders who have open doors while they are on campus, but spend too much time off campus, find their in-office time hurried and stressful. Colleagues accustomed to getting their chair's attention by stopping by the office discover a long line of students and others waiting to get the chair's attention. During office stays, visitors find an individual too burdened with appointments and tasks to pay sufficient attention to the issue at hand. In this way, an open-door policy meant to advertise "I'm here to chat" results in a harried chair without enough time to chat with everyone who seeks his attention.

As an academic leader, your presence on campus is vital. It makes you available to your faculty, staff, students, and administrators. It models behavior indicative of a vibrant and engaged department. It allows you to be responsive to emergencies and happenstance interactions. It also gives you sufficient time to devote to office meetings so that you do not become the harried leader described above. As dean, chair, or director, you should strive to be on campus most of the time, using off-campus work selectively to meet your workload needs.

There is another, usually unforeseen and even unrecognized, downside to an open-door policy. Invariably, some individuals will take greater advantage of your availability than others, stopping by multiple times a week for a tête-à-tête about department matters, the local sports team, or campus gossip.

When you have an open door, faculty *notice* who is in your office. Although you may feel no special allegiance toward the frequent visitor, others will make assumptions about that person's high level of access to you—especially if you are in a department with controversial and divisive issues under discussion. Faculty will assume that the frequent visitor has preferential access to the leader.

An example from my own professional history is illustrative here. As a new assistant professor in a large department, I was grateful for my chair's open door and five-day-a-week presence in the department. At the same time, I did not presume to stop by for an informal chat about anything, whether it be local politics or university policy. Though he would have welcomed my visits, I understood his time to be valuable and his agenda full. I also had more than enough work to complete with my own time in the office.

One or two of my department colleagues did not appear to share these same constraints. One especially frequent visitor was the former department chair, a man of strong convictions about how the department should be run and on controversial initiatives under discussion within the faculty.

By giving so much of his face-time to the former chair, our department head unwittingly broadcast the impression that he was under the former chair's influence. Soon the halls whispered of the unfair power the former chair exercised.

Some faculty developed the impression that the current department chair *must* be unduly influenced by his predecessor. Their evidence was the many hours that the former spent listening to latter's counsel in those frequent office visits we all witnessed. The two could have been swapping recipes for all we knew. The *appearance* of privileged access gave way to an impression that undermined the faculty's confidence in the chair's impartiality.

The problems with an open-door policy enumerated here need not evolve if you are selective in how you implement it. If an open-door policy is important to you, by all means adopt one. Simply beware spending too much time with single individuals, allowing your day to be eaten up by visitors, and giving the impression that certain personalities have unfair access to your time and attention.

By Appointment

The alternate extreme of availability's first seesaw is "by appointment only." This individual is available only to those who have arranged an appointment. Even if the appointment is made that same day, the individual insists that a visitor appear on her calendar. The only exceptions are genuine emergencies, such as an injured student or the eruption of a fight in the corridor.

Using a formal appointment policy and calendar does not come naturally to many academic leaders, especially as they transition from full-time faculty. During their faculty life, they may have used an open-door, or "stop in if I'm here," policy, combined with office hours, to make themselves available to students and colleagues.

Abandoning those practices in favor of an appointment-based policy brings discomfort. They fear others will perceive them as less available at best, or imagining themselves as "too important to sit and chat," at worst. The transition moment is one in which they want to make themselves *more* available, so a shift away from an open door appears to set the wrong tone.

This type of thinking is understandable, but too often leads to the very pitfalls described above. The key to maintaining your accessibility while also protecting your time is designing an availability policy that protects against these threats. A "by appointment" practice can go a long way to achieving these dual goals. Remind yourself frequently that *asking people to make appointments does not make you unavailable.*

A by-appointment policy takes more planning, organization, and discipline than an open-door policy. But it pays off in using your limited time in more efficient and concentrated ways. The first step in adopting a by-appointment practice is to dispel the myth that a leader who insists on appointments is necessarily less accessible than one who maintains an open door. This simply is not true. So long as you adhere to the two essential elements of a successful availability policy—that others find it *easy to make an appointment with you* and that they can *meet with you within the timeframe necessary to address their concerns*—you ensure ready accessibility.

How do you make it easy for others to make an appointment with you? First, announce frequently and clearly the procedure for requesting an appointment. If you have an administrative assistant who keeps your calendar, requestors should contact that individual with the following information:

1. What is the topic of the discussion?
2. How much time do you need?
3. How urgent is this issue? What is the timeframe within which you seek this appointment?
4. Are there any materials the chair/director/dean needs to prepare for this appointment?

Each of these is easily and quickly communicated in an email to the administrative assistant, who can then put the appointment in your calendar. If you do not have an assistant and keep your own calendar, instruct your community in the same informational requests. You will likely have to educate and reeducate some faculty and students, and even administrators, on these guidelines. With time and your persistent instructions, individuals will adopt the practice.

How do you ensure that others can meet with you within the timeframe necessary to address their concerns? This requires that you respond to meeting requests promptly. Indeed, no meeting request (properly submitted) should go more than one working day without a response. This does not mean that you *meet* the individual within one day, but rather that the requestor knows when you can meet with her.

This type of responsiveness is essential to indicate your accessibility and genuine desire to be available. When asked about your availability, your colleagues will respond, "Her door isn't usually open, but I can always get an appointment if I need one."

Your responsibility (or that of your assistant) is to answer the appointment requests and fill them into your calendar in a way that honors the requestors' timeframe but also allows you sufficient time for your work. Some requests will be long-term and general. For example, an assistant professor may request an hour to discuss "my progress toward third-year review." Such an appointment is important, but not urgent. You could schedule it within two weeks' time.

In contrast, another request might come at 7:00 a.m., asking for twenty minutes sometime today to discuss "an urgent personal issue." This appointment is (likely) important and definitely urgent. The faculty member might need to tell you about a health issue that will keep her from teaching classes for the foreseeable future. She may need your advice about a student who emailed that morning about suicidal thoughts. You need to maintain enough open space in your schedule to accommodate such urgent requests.

Blocking out times of the day is a way of making appointments between yourself and the work you need to get done. For example, a self-appointment for "work on course schedule" from 9:30 to 11:00 means that no other appointment can take that slot and you have ninety minutes to dedicate to an essential task. All that is needed is your own discipline to stick to that task during the scheduled block. You then feel a sense of a mission accomplished before taking a meeting with a faculty member scheduled for twenty minutes at 11:00.

Another advantage of scheduled appointments is that you are less likely to feel distracted or resentful of your visitors' time. Open-door visitors sometimes, often unconsciously, assume your open door means you are not busy. They might meander from topics related to the classroom to others concerning their neighbor's rusty fence. When the same individual arrives to your office for her appointment, she will focus on the classroom issue for which she has arranged the appointment. She is less likely to abuse your time in an appointment setting.

Furthermore, when the scheduled time has expired, you have the opportunity to say, "I see our allotted time is up. Thanks for making the appointment and sharing this issue with me." You have a professionally recognized reason for ending the meeting, something the open-door practice lacks. Asking someone to leave an open-door office is often awkward as there is no agreed-on guideline for when a person should leave. A scheduled appointment suffers no such limitation.

Finally, an availability practice that relies on appointments *requires* that you employ an appointment software program. Most colleges and universities use Microsoft's Outlook, which has the benefit of merging with the email system and task-management systems. Whatever your institution uses, take advantage of it. An academic leader in today's higher-ed culture has too many tasks, appointments, and meetings to be able to take in all the requests and manage them with pen and paper. Indeed, scheduling software has multiple tools to help you manage your time. Furthermore, it makes requesting an appointment easy for your colleagues.

MANAGING YOUR ELECTRONIC AVAILABILITY

Electronic communication dominates interpersonal exchange in higher ed. Emails, and increasingly text messages, have replaced telephone calls and in-person meetings for everything from the mundane "heads up" to complex information exchanges.

The benefits of this culture change are enormous. Academic leaders can complete many tasks more quickly via email than they could face-to-face or by phone. Laptop computers and home-based internet means they can do so at any time and without having to be in the office. When confronting the many challenges and pitfalls

Figure 7.2. How Do I Manage My Electronic Availability?

that electronic communication has given rise to, we should not forget these important benefits.

The pitfalls are well known: the individual who feels addicted to email, insisting on checking it multiple times through the day, even on weekends; the student or faculty member who texts at all times of the day and night, expecting a response; the angry screeds from a disgruntled colleague, sent to the entire department and copied to the president; and the faculty member who fails to respond to others' emails but regularly emails the leader when she wants something.

Today's academic leaders need to design not only an on-campus availability policy but an electronic availability policy as well. As in the former, your responsibilities remain to *make it easy for others to reach you* and to *respond within a timeframe necessary to address their concerns*. Email and text provide students, faculty, and administrators literally unlimited means to reach you. Anyone can write you at any time, on any topic, and at any length. You must set the limits by deciding how to manage your reading and responding to those messages. The electronic communication seesaw can help you design your electronic availability practice. It asks, "How often do I read and respond to electronic communication?"

24/7

On one end of the electronic availability seesaw is "twenty-four hours a day, seven days a week." This individual keeps email and text alerts on and answers immediately, sometimes interrupting the activity in which he is engaged at the time. He is often a light sleeper who keeps the cell phone by his bed, sending messages in the wee hours. Although truly *constantly* responsive individuals are rare, those who regularly respond within a few hours of a message's receipt are not. Many argue that without such an attentive email regime, they will soon find themselves hopelessly behind in managing their electronic inbox.

The benefits of a highly responsive electronic availability policy are plentiful. One is that students, faculty, staff, and administrators know they can rely on you for prompt responses. Another is that you are more likely to be prepared for the meetings and tasks that greet you each day, as email is the common vehicle through which meeting agendas and other preparatory material are communicated.

Similarly, the argument cited above that many "round-the-clock" responders provide holds significant merit. Managing email regularly is the best way for many to keep their inbox from overfilling. Furthermore, regular attention to electronic communication means you will not miss an important correspondence, or allow one to become buried in your unread inbox.

The downsides of constant electronic availability are nonetheless important to detail. The most common and important is that it robs you of sustained time dedicated to your many other duties. Research demonstrates that humans cannot genuinely multitask; instead, those who consider themselves multitaskers complete small and discrete tasks sequentially, rather than completing numerous tasks simultaneously, as they imagine.[1] Each time an email or a text message intrudes on your work, it is indeed an interruption, breaking up the flow and momentum you have gained on your previous task. The overall effect is that an individual becomes *less efficient* in managing multiple tasks throughout the day than she would be if she dedicated an uninterrupted hour to each discrete task.

A second disadvantage is that constant electronic availability creates a sort of dependence. Individuals who habituate to checking electronic communications regularly throughout the day find it difficult to break away from the device. The phone or laptop becomes an appendage that works its way into family gatherings, meals, and even professional situations. We all witness the meeting participant who pretends to pay attention to the discussion but is (not so) secretly answering emails on a laptop or phone. Many academic leaders fall prey to this form of electronic addiction.

A third and critical danger of round-the-clock electronic communication is the impression it creates on those in your professional community. For those above you, it suggests that you hold no time sacred for your individual work or personal life. Your willingness to write and to respond to the provost or president at 3:00 a.m. on a Sunday gives them the impression that you consider these working hours. Once you have established this practice, you cannot fault them for expecting your responsiveness at all hours. For those working below you, you create the same impression, inviting faculty, staff, and students to reach out to you around the clock.

You also generate a second, and typically unintended, consequence. Because you are the authority figure, even if you avoid that terminology, you set up the expectation that others must respond to you in kind. You may be awake at midnight and using that time to catch up on emails to your staff. Your staff member, however, perceives that the boss expects a response at the same hour. Happily, academic leaders increasingly include alerts in their email signatures that communicate that they do not expect instant responses, such as "My use of late-night and weekend hours to read email does not mean I expect others to do the same."

During Working Hours Only

The opposite side of this seesaw is a "working hours only" electronic availability policy. This individual is accessible and responsive from 8:00 a.m. to 5:00 p.m. Monday through Friday only. Should he receive an email or text outside of those hours, others understand that he will attend to it once the next work day has commenced.

As with the extreme version of "24/7," few academic leaders take a strict version of "working hours only" practice. But many do make it known that colleagues should not expect them to attend to email and text at night or on the weekends, except in cases of genuine emergency.

The primary benefit of a working-hours practice is that it broadcasts to your professional community that you value your off-campus time. It relieves you of the email barrage that so many academic leaders report spoils too much of their time at home. Furthermore, it role-models a balanced professional and personal life. Faculty and staff take the healthy message from their chair that one is not expected to be working at all hours of every day.

Another upside of limiting your electronic communication to mostly working hours is that it helps you keep perspective about what is important. Email and text contain no filtering mechanism separating the mundane from the critical. Colleagues may write to demand action from you in the heat of a moment, a heat that dissipates by the next morning.

Similarly, you may read a harsh text from your provost at 10:00 p.m., just before looking forward to a good night's rest. Instead, you find yourself awake, stressing about the text and generating a response to the provost in your head. Rarely is this time well spent. Instead, read the text from your office in the morning when you are rested, in your professional space, and when the provost has likely moved on to other topics. Responding in these conditions is immeasurably preferable than to doing so at 11:00 the night before.

The pitfalls of limiting your electronic availability are important, but manageable. The first is that you might miss a genuine emergency. To mitigate this possibility, I recommend the following telephone policy: "I don't read electronic communications outside of working hours. If you have an emergency, *call* me." Your responsibility is to keep your phone with you and in service.

A second potential pitfall is that you discover that working hours provide insufficient time to pay proper attention to your electronic communication. The dean whose calendar is filled with meetings, for example, leaves no time to read, much less respond to, the dozens or more emails that have arrived throughout the day. Such a leader runs the immediate and serious risk of missing, or neglecting, important messages. In the longer term, she risks earning a reputation as an unreliable correspondent, among the most infuriating types of leaders to work with. To avoid this threat, block out time each day on your calendar to dedicate to electronic correspondence.

A third challenge is that your bosses, and even your faculty, may be unhappy with limitations on your availability. Certainly it is your responsibility to know your supervisors' expectations around electronic availability. If you are unsure, ask. It is the exceptionally rare provost or dean who expects you to respond to electronic communications immediately and at all hours.

More commonly, you are expected to respond within twenty-four hours during the work week and to be available by phone in the evenings and weekends in case of emergencies. If your faculty (and rarely, staff) expect you to be available outside of working hours, they have developed an unreasonable expectation. As with your on-campus availability policy, your faculty and staff will quickly adjust to your practices if you regularly and clearly communicate them and hold true to the requirements of an effective strategy: that others can easily reach you and that you are responsive to their needs in an appropriate timeframe.

CHOOSING YOUR POINTS ON THE SEESAWS

On-Campus

You need not choose an availability policy that lies on either extreme of the open-door vs. by-appointment seesaw. You may choose to arrange most of your meetings by appointment but hold office hours in which your open door indicates anyone is welcome to walk in for any reason. You may know of individuals who feel uncomfortable making a formal appointment, but for whom informal meetings with you is important. Office hours are ideal in this case.

Typically, as one advances on the academic hierarchy's ladder, she moves rightward on the seesaw, that is, toward greater dependency on scheduled appointments. Once there, many program directors and department chairs discover the benefits of relying on appointments.

In designing your availability policy, consider the following questions:

- Does my current practice work for me? Do I have enough time to complete my duties?
- Does my current practice work for faculty, staff, and students? Do they have enough access to me and my time? Do they feel I am accessible?
- What changes are necessary to make myself sufficiently available but also with enough time for my work and personal life?

Once you have decided on your practice, *overcommunicate* it to your community. Write it outside your door. Announce it multiple times in faculty meetings. If individuals are accustomed to your open door, remind them that you now ask for appointments. Few will begrudge you such a change once you have joined the leadership ranks. And most will adjust more quickly than you imagine.

Also remember that you should generate opportunities to meet with your faculty and staff outside of formally scheduled meetings and appointments. Informal discussions are important. They simply do not have to occur in your office whenever someone gets the impulse to stop by. Department lunches, coffees, potlucks, and happy hours can be productive opportunities for exchanges that are meaningful, though not very formal.

For example, you might set up one lunch per month to which all faculty are invited. Advertise that there is no agenda other than to listen to what people would like to talk about. Similarly, you might host a tea for assistant professors, or for the faculty in a particular subfield. These types of get-togethers often draw individuals who would neither make an appointment with you nor stop by your open door. But a group lunch might be the perfect forum in which they feel most comfortable to share their experience and point of view.

Electronic

As with your on-campus availability, neither extreme of the electronic-availability seesaw is likely to best suit your needs. Most leaders lean too heavily on a "round-the-clock" electronic response practice, robbing themselves of personal and professional time, and modeling a poor work-life balance to their colleagues. That said, there are few more frustrating individuals in higher ed than the director, chair, or dean who fails to respond to email. Email is the primary currency of interprofessional communication in the academy. As such, your co-workers deserve your prompt attention.

The question thus becomes, *What is a reasonable timeframe within which to respond to electronic communication?* The answer varies across institutions, and you know best your university's culture. Twenty-four hours, or the next business day, is an appropriate starting point in designing your policy. This means that you respond within one day (or the next business day for messages that arrive on Friday or the weekend) to communications that require a response. Such a policy ensures that you answer promptly, but allows you to turn off the text and email alerts that interrupt your meetings and work throughout the day.

Twenty-four hours is also a suitable amount of time for you to cool off from your reactions to angry and unprofessional correspondence in your inbox. The cool-down period not only provides time to generate an appropriate response but also insures you against writing your own emotionally laden retort that you later regret.

It is possible that you may need variable practices for different people in your professional life. For example, you may work for a provost or president who expects you to respond immediately to electronic communication. Failure to do so could jeopardize your good standing. In such a case, take advantage of our electronic devices' features to set alerts only for incoming messages from those individuals. And resist making the same unreasonable expectations of those who work for you.

In finding your place on the electronic-availability seesaw, remember the goals and criteria laid out at the beginning of this chapter. You seek a policy that meets your dual objectives of completing your work and having time to yourself. And your practice needs to meet your colleagues' need for ease of access and hearing back from you in a reasonable timeframe. Different leaders can well achieve these objectives with varying policies.

Finally, it is as essential to overcommunicate your electronic-availability policy as it is your on-campus policy. Announce your policy in a department meeting and follow up with an email and in the minutes. You might say, "You can expect me to respond within 24 hours, or by the next business day, to your electronic communication. I ask for the same from you. Of course, in case of emergency, we should call each other directly." Frequent reiteration of this policy will pay off in bringing your team on board to this practice.

Being available to faculty, staff, and students is one of the academic leader's most important responsibilities. Without it, you lose touch with those you serve. Too few leaders think seriously about their strategy for time management, and thus, their availability to their constituents. This often causes leaders to be overwhelmed by the needs of individuals who demand a lot of attention. This leads to insufficient time dedicated to the many duties of the job, which in turn can cause them to display impatience or lack of attention during those times individuals are in their office. The availability seesaws provide a framework to help you be accessible to your professional community—both in person and electronically—while preserving healthy blocks of time for yourself.

ESSENTIAL IDEAS IN THIS CHAPTER

- Academics who take on leadership positions should create a plan for managing their on-campus and electronic availability. The practices that work for a faculty member rarely work for a leader.
- Two essential criteria drive your availability strategies: (1) individuals must be able to easily contact you, and (2) you must respond within the necessary time to address individuals' concerns.
- Many academic leaders find that an "open-door" policy generates more problems than it solves.
- Asking individuals to make an appointment with you does not mean that you are unavailable, but that your time is valuable.
- An appointment-management software is essential for enacting productive and efficient availability plans.
- Round-the-clock attention to electronic communication is common among academic leaders, but it is rarely necessary or helpful.

- A promise to respond to electronic communication within twenty-four hours is a reasonable policy.
- Once you have created your availability plan, overcommunicate it to all the constituencies with whom you interact.

NOTE

1. N. Yeung and S. Monsell, "Switching between Tasks of Unequal Familiarity: The Role of Stimulus-Attribute and Response-Set Selection," Journal of Experimental Psychology—Human Perception and Performance 29, no. 2 (2003) : 455–69; L. Gopher, L. Armony, and Y. Greenspan, "Switching Tasks and Attention Policies," Journal of Experimental Psychology: General 129 (2000): 308–29.

EIGHT

Focus of Attention

between problems & opportunities [handwritten annotation]

As important as managing your time is managing your *focus*. Academic leaders invariably have a multitude of demands on their time and attention on any given day. Over the course of a school year, you must devote your attention to many problems, complaints, and challenges that are both acute and chronic in nature. For example, you need to respond both to the angry parent demanding a return phone call and to that chronically underenrolled course.

Although putting out these and hundreds of other fires could consume most of your time, you should give fair time and energy to the opposite of fires—your unit's successes and opportunities. These, too, are both immediate and long-term. For example, you should announce and celebrate a faculty member's grant award shortly after she receives the news. Similarly, you must dedicate time to nurturing your department's reputation for excellence in teaching and advising. The problems and challenges often draw us in, but we must remember to cultivate the positives all around us.

The two focus-of-attention seesaws aim to help you to understand and adjust your patterns to manage the voluminous incoming challenges and opportunities facing every academic leader. The first seesaw asks, "<u>What</u> draws your attention?" The second examines <u>who</u> draws your attention. Inspecting your own tendencies in each area will help ensure that you are not avoiding particular issues and people who need your consideration. Effective academic leaders strike a balance between focusing on problems and opportunities, as well as between individuals who are squeaky wheels and silent types.

It is especially important to scrutinize our choices in these areas, as they are especially vulnerable to following our internal default settings. What comes most naturally may not be the most effective response in any given situation.

WHAT DRAWS YOUR ATTENTION?

The first focus-of-attention seesaw varies from "problems" to "successes." Problem-focused leaders tend to see what's not working and seek to rectify it. When evaluating a plan of action, they see elements that fail, even when most components succeed. They experience stress when faculty and staff underperform or undermine the unit's accomplishments. Some are perfectionists who find it difficult to appreciate a job well done when even a tiny aspect of that job did not live up to their expectations. They are comfortable pointing out what is wrong and in holding people accountable. They are "glass half empty" leaders.

On the other end of this spectrum are those who many characterize as optimists. They are more comfortable celebrating what is working than in condemning what is not. Even when an initiative

Figure 8.1.   What Draws My Attention?

has failed to live up to its promise, they congratulate individuals on those parts that achieved some success. Problems and complaints generate little stress for them, so they are less likely to chastise faculty and staff for underperformance. These "glass half full" leaders typically have a positive point of view and enjoy a reputation as supportive of their team.

It is tempting to denounce the problem-oriented leader and praise the success-oriented leader. We suspect we would prefer to work for the latter. It is important, however, to point out that leaders inhabiting either end of this seesaw can fall into equally dangerous traps.

The failings of a strongly problem-oriented leader are well known and revolve around team management and employee satisfaction. Such a leader inspires fear and dismay in team members. They work hard toward a goal, yet their supervisor's only recognition is critique. They become fixated on avoiding errors, a practice that leaves genuine productivity and creativity little space to flourish.

By hearing so frequently what is *wrong,* faculty and staff miss the equally important feedback concerning what is *right.* Employees need to learn both which activities and behavior to avoid and which to emulate. The problem-focused leader acknowledges only the former. Work under a leader with this orientation is rarely a happy place. Burnout is common, and team members likely commiserate often about the mean boss. The leader may gain a reputation for a unit that rarely commits egregious errors, but he unlikely oversees a productive and long-serving team.

In contrast, the leader who focuses nearly exclusively on successes typically oversees a unit that underperforms. Whereas *personnel* is the issue with the problem-oriented leader, the *work product* is more often under threat with the success-oriented leader. This leader develops a reputation for accolades, backslaps, and frequent enunciations of "good job!" He goes out of his way to praise faculty and staff for their hard work, but rarely distinguishes between those who truly work hard and those who do not.

Units under this individual's leadership have little incentive, and even less direction, aiming them toward a standard of excellence. Lacking that direction, and buoyed by perpetual accolades, faculty and staff rarely live up to their greatest promise and instead deliver underwhelming results.

Work product most commonly suffers under extreme versions of the success-oriented leader. There are also two important and personnel-related dangers. First, this leader avoids pointing out individuals' errors and failures to perform up to standard. In so doing, she risks giving people the misimpression that they are on track for a positive annual evaluation, a merit raise, and even promotion and tenure. They understandably feel deceived when they receive a less-than-stellar annual evaluation, raise, or promotion decision.

A department chair's unwillingness to identify weaknesses and failures in candidates' performance can make it impossible to deny them tenure and promotion later, even if they fail to meet the institution's expectations. The candidate rightly asks, "If I wasn't meeting the standards all these years, why didn't my chair tell me?"

The second personnel-related danger under a success-oriented leader is that truly exceptional performers go without the congratulations they merit. Academic departments rely heavily on faculty members' self-motivation, willingness to volunteer, and sense of commitment to the department's overall success. Deans and department heads have few tools to reward high performance. This makes public affirmation and accolades all the more important in recognizing those who do their jobs especially well.

The chair who praises everyone, despite genuine differences in their contributions and productivity, risks burnout and resentment among her genuinely exceptional faculty. They rightly conclude that their above-and-beyond efforts earn no more recognition than those of colleagues who put in half the work.

WHO DRAWS YOUR ATTENTION?

As important in reflecting on how you delegate your attention among problems and success is your approach to the people you manage. The second focus-of-attention seesaw examines who gets your attention and to whose cues you respond. On one end are the squeaky wheels. On the other are the silent types. Despite the fact that the former demands your attention and the latter does not, *both* types and everyone in between require your focus.

The squeaky wheel gets the grease is a truism in professional life inside and outside the Academy. In personnel management, the squeaky wheel typically suggests a complainer or an egotist who demands attention whether he deserves it or not. Certainly, chairs and deans see plenty of squeaky wheels. There are belligerent individuals with a host of complaints and daily entreaties they insist be addressed immediately, regardless of their accuracy or import. Sim-

Squeaky Wheels

Silent Types

Figure 8.2.   Who Draws My Attention?

ilarly, some faculty who behave as *prima donnas* insist that you reward and praise them, even though what they imagine to be exceptional performance does not compare favorably with that of colleagues.

Yet some squeaky wheels have legitimate concerns, complaints, and requests for attention. The staff member who reports weekly that the registration system is failing draws your attention to a true crisis that demands your immediate attention. Similarly, very high performers often become squeaky wheels in their pursuit of your recognition of their success. If the department head fails to celebrate individuals' specific successes, those individuals conclude that they must squeak in pursuit of any acknowledgement. Their appeals to you for recognition may annoy, but your failure to publicly applaud their achievements necessitates their squeaky behavior.

Define the squeaky wheel not automatically as an irritant and complainer, but rather simply as one who brings issues to your attention. Sometimes those issues are valid and important, other times less so. Some squeaky wheels communicate them in professionally appropriate ways, other times in self-serving and bombastic ways. In either case, you must focus on the *content* of the issue, rather than on the individual or its method of delivery.

The opposite of the squeaky wheel is the silent type—those individuals who rarely, if ever, bring matters to your attention. Amidst the hectic days of academic leadership, leaders typically feel grateful for their silent types. By demanding no attention and seeming to go about their work without need for the leader's acclamation, the silent types make running a department or college easier.

For our purposes, then, the left side of the seesaw finds the leader attentive to squeaky wheels and in danger of ignoring the silent types. On the right side is the leader who is particularly sensitive to the quiet types in the unit and adept at resisting those who demand attention.

It is the rare academic leader who finds herself on the silent-type end of this seesaw. A leader balancing heavily toward the silent types treats the squeaky wheels almost as parents behave toward a toddler who acts out to attract attention. The advice goes that you ignore all attention-seeking behaviors, thereby teaching the toddler that his squeaks will go ungreased. In the meantime, you shower attention on the other children who do not demand it, thereby illustrating to the toddler that the best way to get your attention is to play nicely.

Played out in an academic department setting, this scenario has the chair ignoring squeaky wheels' emails and tirades. Instead, the chair deliberately seeks out the quieter faculty, inquiring as to how their work is going, offering support, and celebrating their achievements in private and in public. Such an approach may dissuade the squeaky wheel, but it could also rob you of important information the squeaky seeks to convey.

With so many tasks to be completed in the day, and so many squeaky wheels demanding our attention, it is exceptionally difficult to spend much time on the silent-type end of the seesaw. Much more common are the department head and dean who focus on the squeaky wheels, too many of whom are difficult and unfairly insistent on their leaders' time.

Tilting too heavily toward the squeaky-wheel end of the seesaw carries some important dangers. Just as the leader who emphasizes successes at the cost of problems runs the risk of alienating her high-performers, the leader who pays inordinate attention to the squeaky wheel risks the resentment of the silent types. They understandably learn the lesson that the "well-behaved" toddler does in the house where the brat gets all the parents' attention: "In order for my chair to recognize me, I have to shout and make demands. My strong performance and collegial behavior are not enough." This, of course, is the opposite of the message most leaders want to send.

A less visible danger in avoiding the silent types is that you fail to notice those with weaknesses. A silent type who avoids drawing your attention may do so in hopes that you fail to notice he is a mediocre teacher, never participates in committee meetings, or has disengaged from scholarly activity. It can also feel more difficult to confront the silent type, because he never makes any trouble in the department. As the academic leader, nonetheless, you are responsible for upholding your department's standards of performance, even for the silent types whom you secretly appreciate because they are undemanding.

CHOOSING YOUR POINTS ON THE SEESAWS

For some of the balancing acts we have reviewed so far, you can successfully choose a lopsided point on the seesaw because it is the appropriate choice for your leadership style and institutional context. For example, you might fall strongly on the "open door" availability continuum and remain productive and effective.

On the focus-of-attention seesaws, you need to choose a point more toward the middle than at either extreme. A leader whose focus rarely veers from the squeaky wheels and the unit's problems misses opportunities and responsibilities lying among the silent types and the unit's successes. The reverse is true as well.

A helpful metaphor for finding your balance is that of the "health and wellness specialist." For centuries, Western medicine emphasized *illness*, in other words, what was wrong with an individual's health. In recent years, a focus on *wellness* has emerged. Wellness emphasizes what is right with an individual's health. Illness requires a fix, a treatment, an intervention, and a cure. Wellness requires support, recognition, maintenance, and planning for sustained health.

Today's medical professionals increasingly speak of health *and* wellness. In so doing, they balance fixing what is wrong with maintaining what is right. Similarly, a healthy balance on the focus-of-attention seesaws sees the academic leader known for celebrating accomplishments, even among the silent types, but unafraid in addressing problems and challenges.

As was suggested in chapter 6's discussion on your leadership comfort zone, begin your focus-of-attention work by asking yourself questions aimed at identifying where your attentions lie. Do I respond to problems as soon as they emerge? Do I go out of my way to praise successes? Do I allow the squeaky wheels to take up a disproportionate amount of my time and attention? Have I reached out to the silent types in my unit? Do my notes from meetings with faculty and administration show that I'm talking about successes or problems? In conversations with my dean and provost, do I remember to celebrate my department's achievements as much as I commiserate about its weaknesses?

Once you have engaged in this type of self-examination, ask others how they perceive you. Seek out the silent types and inquire whether they feel you pay them sufficient attention. Engage your faculty in a brief feedback exercise in which you share images of the focus-of-attention seesaws and ask, "Where do you see me falling on these seesaws?" and "What adjustments would you like me to make?" As always, faculty feedback alone should not determine your decision, but it should be an important contribution.

Table 8.1 presents a summary of the dangers associated with leaning too heavily toward either end of the focus-of-attention seesaws. The table identifies some typical faculty types at the intersection of the two focus-of-attention seesaws: what and on whom you focus. Let us consider first the "successes." These are faculty (and staff) who perform their duties at or above your expectations. They reliably deliver in teaching, scholarship, and service. In other words, they are high performers.

Among these high performers are some silent types who often go *overlooked* by their department chair or dean, for reasons described above. They are in danger of receiving less attention, compensation, and congratulations than they deserve. You should regularly survey your faculty and staff for the potentially overlooked. They are often your most collegial and productive team members.

Also found among the high performers are squeaky wheels. These are the *self-promoters*. They enjoy the advantage of real achievements backing up their self-congratulations. The danger to their supervisor is that they receive more than their share of accolades because their self-promotion is successful. The prima donnas in our ranks often fall into this category. They are high achievers, and want to make sure everyone knows it.

Table 8.1.

	Successes	Problems
Silent Types	Often overlooked	Fly under the radar
Squeaky Wheels	Self-promoters	Deluded or diverter

Turning now to the "problems." These are faculty (and staff) who either underperform or behave unprofessionally, or both. Underperformers might be poor teachers, those who have abandoned a research program, or terrible academic advisors. The unprofessionals include those who bully colleagues, gossip about department politics with students, engage in research misconduct, or cancel class frequently.

The problem faculty who are also silent types run the danger of *flying under your radar*. As discussed above, you might fail to notice their behavior because they tend to keep quiet. You must pay special attention to their indicators of productivity and performance, because they rarely bring these to your attention.

The squeaky wheels who are also underperformers or unprofessionals typically present our most difficult cases. They are either *deluded* or *diverters*. The deluded genuinely misjudge their own performance. They imagine themselves magnificent teachers, when in fact they simply tell stories from the podium while students sit in bored frustration. The diverters are aware of, and nervous about, their own sub-par performance, so they seek to distract your attention. They complain about others, exaggerate some long-ago achievement, and promote their own importance as the "department historian" to keep you from noticing their weak performance.

Consider the types in table 8.1. Do any of your faculty meet these profiles? If so, you can begin to adjust your attention profile. *Each member* of your faculty and staff deserves your attention. Similarly, your responsibility as an academic leader is to pay appropriate attention to your unit's success stories and to its shortcomings. Thinking carefully about your points on the focus-of-attention seesaws can help you to strike the proper balances.

ESSENTIAL IDEAS IN THIS CHAPTER

- Effective academic leaders should pay close attention to the people and issues that attract their attention.
- Find an effective balance between problem-focus and success-focus.
- Overemphasis on celebrating successes can leave important problems unaddressed.
- Overemphasis on fixing problems can leave your staff and faculty feeling unappreciated and demoralized.

- Balance your attention among your squeaky wheels, your silent types, and others in between.
- Squeaky wheels often demand more of your attention than they deserve, but they should not be discounted entirely.
- Silent types may be the most productive workers, but they receive the least attention.
- Both squeaky wheels and silent types can manipulate their behavior to divert your attention from their performance weaknesses.
- An effective academic leader will find a balance in the middle of the focus-of-attention seesaws.

NINE

Feedback

as needed — at least weekly

Many department chairs and program directors, and even some deans, find providing formal feedback to their faculty and staff the most challenging of their assigned responsibilities. Most easily and generously offer praise and positive reinforcement. Articulating performance weaknesses, however, comes as a struggle. The result is that American higher education is replete with departments where meaningful feedback goes missing for years and even decades.

A chair's feedback system is often the most important component in how faculty and staff feel about their leader. It communicates much more than a simple grading of performance. It is a measure of the leader's care, thoughtfulness, honesty, fairness and communication style. All of these profoundly influence the degree to which faculty and staff respect and admire their chair.

WHY DO ACADEMIC LEADERS SO OFTEN FAIL TO PROVIDE NEGATIVE FEEDBACK?

Numerous aspects of academic culture contribute to an environment within which holding underperformers accountable is especially difficult. First, the academy is defined as a collegial workplace. Although it certainly has hierarchies, they are less rigid than in most workplaces. All faculty enjoy the same rights and freedoms, regardless of their rank or title. Most value the community spirit that permeates academic culture. Academic leaders sometimes feel that critical feedback of a colleague violates that collegial atmosphere.

A second aspect working against honest feedback of underperformers is that very few academic leaders receive any training in evaluation best practices. Honest, clear, and sometimes negative feedback is *hard* to give. The leadership literature is replete with models, suggestions, and procedures about how to do it well.[1]

Most university human resources (HR) offices offer resources and workshops on this topic. Still, too few leaders, especially at the academic department level, engage in meaningful professional development around feedback and evaluation. Without training in this hardest of tasks, most chairs and directors soft pedal their critiques of faculty underperformance.

Conflict avoidance is another obstacle you might experience in attempting to provide meaningful feedback to your faculty and staff. Most of us prefer to avoid conflict, especially within a typically collegial and friendly department. Delivering negative feedback to a colleague feels like (and often is) an invitation to conflict with that individual. When performed professionally and via best practices, however, it need not be painful for you or the faculty member. More importantly, by offering honest feedback, you provide the employee the information he needs to improve his performance and grow professionally.

Another challenge to critical feedback is experienced especially by chairs and directors who plan to return to the department faculty after their term in leadership. Most department heads do not retire in that position, but rather return to faculty for some time after their leadership term. Revolving-chair systems, in which all members take their leadership "turn," assures this situation. As is discussed in chapter 1, department heads often worry that if they hold a faculty member accountable for her underperformance, that same individual will exact retribution on them when she becomes chair in the future.

A final reality that keeps many academic leaders from giving honest and critical feedback is the lack of a support structure to back them up. Time and again, department heads and deans report that their efforts to write meaningful, and sometimes critical, evaluations are undercut by those above them in the institutional hierarchy. This lack of support is devastating, both because it makes it more difficult to manage the unit and because it undermines your confidence in your institution's senior leadership.

I have yet to meet a provost, dean, or HR official who admits to undermining his department heads and school deans. Yet there are many common behaviors and policies that do just that. Schools that lack merit pay and post-tenure evaluation, for example, rob their academic leaders of meaningful instruments to hold faculty accountable. The offender bears no consequences other than a poor evaluation from the chair or director. The typical result is that the offender resents the messenger (department head) and pays little attention to the message (performance problems). In such an environment, many chairs decide the costs of providing negative feedback are too high.

A second example of poor support structure is when the human resources professionals and/or the senior academic leadership fail to back a courageous chair who provides a negative faculty assessment. Some senior leaders blame the tenure system for failure to support a chair or dean: "I know he's bad at his job, but he's tenured. There's nothing we can do." Such a statement is not only cowardly but also inaccurate.

Tenure is not designed to protect faculty no matter how weak their performance. That so many universities treat tenure as a guarantee against meaningful performance evaluations does not negate the fact that institutions can (and sometimes do) hold tenured faculty accountable for underperforming in their jobs or unprofessional behavior.

A third, and especially unkind, way senior leaders undermine courageous chairs and deans is when they give a friendly ear to the offender. Certainly HR professionals and provosts must listen to faculty complaints, including those about perceived unfair evaluations from their department heads. Too often, however, persistently difficult or underperforming faculty succeed in getting a higher-up to withdraw or otherwise mitigate the effects of a negative evaluation. This, of course, leaves the department head not only undermined but also in an even weaker position than where he started vis-à-vis the problem faculty member. Furthermore, it is especially dispiriting to discover that your supervisor does not back you up after you stuck your neck out to do the right thing for your department.

These aspects of academic culture certainly can make it harder to provide honest and sometimes critical evaluations to your faculty and staff. This notwithstanding, providing accurate and timely feedback is among your most important duties. Without it, you cannot fairly expect the high performers to feel recognized and appreciated, or the low performers to make improvements. It is therefore unfair to both the high and low performers. Genuine performance assessment is essential for individuals' professional growth and the department's or school's path to success.

Two distinct seesaws examine your feedback practices. The first concerns the *type* of feedback you provide. The second concerns the *frequency* with which you provide it.

FEEDBACK TYPE

What type of feedback do you provide? In other words, what is the nature of its content? This seesaw varies from one extreme of "only positive" to the other of "only negative." As with the focus-of-attention seesaw, the effective leader falls on neither extreme on this seesaw but must instead strike the proper balance between positive and negative feedback.

The "always and only positive" leader tends to be conflict-avoidant and uncomfortable pointing out deficiencies in a colleague's performance or behavior. In written and oral evaluations, she accentuates what the individual does well and simply omits areas in need of remediation. Such a leader is frequently well-liked, because she generates little conflict and is perceived as highly supportive of her team.

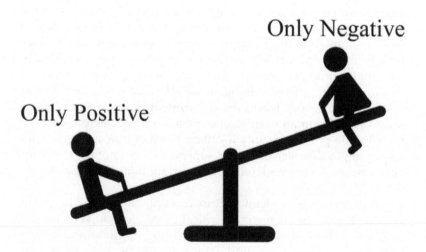

Figure 9.1. What Type of Feedback Do You Give?

At the same time, the always-positive leader can draw resentment and criticism. This comes especially from those genuinely high-performers who feel their success goes without meaningful acknowledgment and that the underperformers suffer no consequences or accountability for their behavior.

The "always and only negative" evaluator is similar to the "problem-oriented" manager discussed in chapter 8. He focuses on individuals' weaknesses and areas for improvement, too often forgetting to detail individuals' successes. Such a leader is rarely popular among faculty and staff, who feel that they can never do enough to please.

Here too, the high performers are particularly frustrated because they experience the same type of (negative) attention from their leader as the underperformers do. Furthermore, because strong work goes unrecognized, individuals have little incentive to "keep up the good work." Their supervisor has not identified what "good work" looks like. Departments working under only negative leaders tend to be fearful and unhappy places to work, often with high turnover.

In the academy today, there are few academic leaders on either extreme of this seesaw, though the "only positive" certainly outnumber the "only negative." Your task in evaluation is to provide an accurate assessment. For the vast majority of your faculty and staff, that will contain *both* positive and negative elements—areas of success and areas for improvement.

FEEDBACK FREQUENCY

In thinking about feedback for faculty and staff, we tend to focus on *formal* feedback. This typically comes in the form of annual performance evaluations, as well as promotion and tenure assessments. These are of course essential, but they typically form only a fraction of the feedback you provide.

Throughout any given year, most academic leaders employ conversations, announcements, emails, notes, and other forms of communication to offer compliments or criticism to individuals. It is important to recognize and exploit these informal messages as components of your feedback practices.

On one extreme of the feedback-frequency seesaw is "once a year." This chair waits until the conclusion of the academic year to

Once a Year

Daily

Figure 9.2.   How Frequently Do You Give Feedback?

evaluate individuals' performance, and does so only in the formal annual evaluation.

The effects of the once-a-year practice present challenges to both the evaluator and the recipient. The evaluator has to collect and remember all the data needed for the annual evaluation from throughout the year. He may have indices like teaching evaluations and research output at his disposal. However, elements such as contributions in faculty meetings, class observations, committee service, and other performance components are not easily summarized in objective form. And he is unlikely to remember accurately many of the faculty member's activities and contributions that do not fit neatly in annual activities report.

The faculty or staff member who receives feedback only once a year spends twelve months without any knowledge from the chair about her performance. Especially if the annual evaluation contains criticisms, she rightly wishes that she had been alerted sooner, so she could have worked to address the problems. In cases where the evaluation emerges as highly positive, the employee may similarly wish the chair had let her know she was doing a good job. That would have averted the stress of not knowing whether she performed up to expectations.

At the other extreme is the leader who offers feedback constant-ly. This leader makes sure to visit each faculty and staff member daily, offering everything from "keep up the good work!" to "I see your assessment report has not been submitted." Working under this feedback style, faculty and staff have the benefit of constant awareness of how their leader feels about them. They also likely resent that the leader gives them too little space and time to com-plete their jobs as independent professionals.

The constant-feedback-provider who errs toward positive com-mentary runs the risk of being perceived as obsequious and even insecure. In contrast, the leader who delivers a constant stream of usually negative feedback earns the reputation as a micromanager, the type of supervisor few employees enjoy working for.

An effective academic leader falls on neither of these feedback-frequency extremes. Rather, she is quick to offer congratulations for achievements and to address concerns as they arise. She uses multi-ple methods of communication—public acknowledgments, congrat-ulatory emails, in-office conversations—to provide feedback throughout the year. She also writes detailed and accurate annual reviews. Because she has provided other types of feedback through-out the year, the annual evaluation contains no surprises. Rather, it summarizes most of what the individual already knows.

CHOOSING YOUR POINTS ON THE SEESAW

As with all the balancing acts introduced in this book, begin your feedback choices with an honest audit of your current practices. What type of feedback do you typically share—positive or nega-tive? How often do you provide it and in what form? Do you vary your communication style, or do you always rely on, for example, email?

Once you have completed this self-audit, ask some of your direct reports about how they experience your feedback practices. Do they understand your assessment of their performance? Do they receive feedback promptly, or do they have to wait until annual evalua-tions? Do they feel you both celebrate their successes and point out their failures?

Your overall strategy for feedback is to strike an appropriate balance between positive and negative, frequent and annual. You should also tailor your feedback regime to different individuals' professional styles and needs. Some employees crave feedback and assume the worst if they do not receive frequent accolades from their supervisor. Others find receiving feedback awkward, even stressful, so prefer to receive it less regularly.

Similarly, individuals' performance profiles vary and thus require different feedback practices from you. Those new to the job and on a steep learning curve may need you to check in regularly to ensure that they are on track. Others with complete mastery of their duties likely need little feedback. Those with performance weaknesses need quick and often regular interventions while high performers merit only an occasional "good job!"

Table 9.1 documents some of the behaviors expressed by supervisors who fall too strongly toward the extremes of the feedback seesaws. The academic leader who offers only praise and does so constantly is a *conflict avoider*. He seeks to build a bulwark against criticism of him and his leadership by fawning about everyone's great performance, regardless of whether it is merited.

Such a practice often feels good to the department at the start, but quickly becomes revealed for what it is. The leader then develops a reputation for not standing up to difficult and underperforming faculty. He can also appear obsequious, as if exaggerating his kindness in search of approval. Furthermore, he does a disservice to truly high performers for failing to distinguish between their behavior and that of others.

In contrast, the academic leader who provides only positive feedback but does so exclusively at annual evaluations is likely to be *disengaged*. This individual writes an annual evaluation that is all congratulatory but has failed to even acknowledge those same achievements throughout the year. Furthermore, any performance failures go unmentioned in the annual review.

These behaviors suggest a leader who cares too little about faculty and staff work throughout the year to offer any accolades, and who is too lazy to engage in the difficult work of critiquing individuals for their shortcomings. Universities' files are replete with annual evaluations claiming that faculty and staff "exceeded expectations" in all categories, when in fact they did not. Not only is this

Table 9.1.

	All Positive	All Negative
Constant	Conflict avoider	Micromanager/evil boss
Once a Year	Disengaged	The ambush

unfair to the leader's successor who tries to complete meaningful evaluations in a culture accustomed to "everyone is great all the time," but it is also unfair to current faculty and staff, who deserve honesty from their supervisor.

For those (rare) academic leaders who offer only criticism, the one who does so constantly is a *micromanager*, and likely has earned a reputation as an evil boss. No one enjoys working for someone who not only hovers over them but also only offers disapproval and never praise. Happily, these leaders are very rare in higher education, especially in academic departments.

The supervisor who leaves all feedback to the annual evaluation and then provides only or mostly criticism runs the risk of launching an *ambush*. Faculty and staff who receive no feedback throughout the year understandably work with the assumption that their performance meets expectations. To learn in their annual evaluation that their performance in fact *fails* to meet expectations not only comes as a surprise but also feels unfair. They rightly argue that had they been notified of problems earlier, they would have addressed them. Now their performance problem is documented in an annual evaluation, and they have less time to ameliorate it. Faculty and staff have the right not to be subject to an ambush. As their supervisor, even if you prefer to avoid conflict, you owe it to them to point out shortcomings when they arise.

Study table 9.1 and consider your feedback practices. Do you find any evidence that you fall into any of these feedback types? If so, consider both the type and frequency feedback seesaws to move toward a better balance in your evaluation regime. The feedback type and frequency seesaws are ones in which you strive toward a balance between the extremes. Recalling that evaluating your colleagues is probably the hardest part of your job, reach out to HR and other opportunities for professional development. There are abundant templates and best practices available to help you.

ESSENTIAL IDEAS IN THIS CHAPTER

- Multiple aspects of academic culture undermine academic leaders' ability and willingness to provide meaningful performance feedback, especially when it is negative.
- Effective academic leaders pay careful attention to both the type and frequency of the feedback they provide.

- Faculty and staff need feedback on their strengths and weaknesses, successes, and failures.
- Once-a-year feedback does not constitute a meaningful or effective evaluation system.
- Leaders whose feedback does not strike an even balance on both the type and frequency seesaws run the risk of alienating their faculty and staff and failing to improve overall performance.

NOTE

1. Jeffrey I. Buller, *Best Practices in Faculty Evaluation: A Practical Guide for Academic Leaders* (San Francisco: Jossey-Bass, 2012); Raoul A. Arreola, *Developing a Comprehensive Faculty Evaluation System: A Guide to Designing, Building, and Operating Large-Scale Faculty Evaluation Systems*, 3rd ed. (San Francisco: Jossey-Bass, 2006); Peter Seldin, *Evaluating Faculty Performance: A Practical Guide to Assessing Teaching, Research, and Service* (San Francisco: Jossey-Bass, 2006).

TEN

Balance the Seesaws, and Tailor Your Leadership

The eight seesaws presented in this book may appear overwhelming, especially to new or aspiring academic leaders. You may be thinking, "How can I possibly deliberate on each of these balancing acts as I approach every situation, person, and decision facing me?" Incorporating the seesaws into your leadership practices will take some time and effort. Developing any new habit does. But you will quickly discover that the self-awareness and careful thinking that the seesaw exercises demand make your decision-making clearer, your tactics more efficient, and your actions more enduring.

Begin by choosing the seesaws that strike you as most helpful and urgent. For example, if you struggle with time management, begin with the availability seesaw (chapter 7). If you feel constant tension between your faculty and administrator roles, start with the identity and role seesaws (chapters 2 and 3). If you are a new leader working to build a healthy culture within your unit, the seesaws on leadership comfort zone, decision-making style, and management style (chapters 4, 5, and 6) will be especially important to get started on the right foot.

The seesaws are both a *habit* and a *tool*. Habituate yourself to thinking about the many tradeoffs that the seesaws represent as you go through your busy days and weeks of interacting with colleagues, making decisions, leading change, supporting excellence, and remediating problems. You face an enormous diversity of tasks.

The seesaw approach helps you navigate through that complexity and arrive at the best leadership approach for each situation.

Develop a *seesaw mindset*, one in which the balancing acts become part of your daily thinking and approach. You will know you have gained a new habit when you discover yourself naturally asking, "What elements and priorities do I need to balance in this situation?" as you take on new assignments. You will gain a reputation for taking care before making a decision, responding to a challenge, or managing a tricky personnel case.

At the same time, each seesaw is a specific tool that can frame your deep thinking about how to best approach a challenge or opportunity. On issues involving major change or controversial topics, finding the right balance on the seesaw can be the difference between success and failure. Consider, for example, some of the major questions facing deans, department heads, and program directors today: Will we close low-enrolled programs? How do we insert professional skills into our liberal-arts core curriculum? How will we handle budget cuts and declining revenues? Your ability to approach, manage, and lead on these and other critical issues will determine your success as an academic leader.

Each of existential challenges, and many more, tap directly and deeply into the heart of what higher education means to faculty, staff, and students. Passions rise, tempers flare, fears are expressed, accusations are thrown. The academic leader who carefully decides where to locate on the identity, role, and management-style seesaws greatly enhances her chance of leading the faculty through these difficult scenarios. One who does not runs the risk of leading only with his dominant leadership style, which may be ill-suited to these highly charged tasks.

The remainder of this chapter summarizes the content in the book. It encapsulates the major themes, lessons, tools, and advice. You can use it as a primer to refresh your understanding of its contributions and get you back toward using the seesaw approach in your leadership.

MANAGING THE BALANCING ACT: THEMES AND LESSONS

1. Embrace Your Leadership

Academic culture in the United States devalues leadership in both obvious and subtle ways. Faculty who pursue a position as department head, associate dean, or dean are too often chided for moving to the "dark side" or criticized for spending less time on scholarship and teaching. This is deeply unfortunate. Higher education faces multiple and existential crises. Intramural tensions between faculty and administration make the leadership landscape especially treacherous. Enthusiastic and expert leadership is more important than ever before. We should nurture, train, support, and celebrate all who aspire to and take on academic leadership positions. Academic leaders should be aware of, and not fall prey to, a culture that seeks to undermine their pride in leadership.

2. No Single Set of Traits Guarantees Leadership Success

Too many people, search committees, and even leaders themselves argue that successful leaders embody a set of essential traits and that absence of those traits makes for a poor leader. This belief not only collapses under scrutiny but also likely discourages potential leaders who worry they do not possess the special mix of leadership attributes. Furthermore, many of the purported "must haves" for leadership success actually contradict one another—for example, good listener vs. bold decision-maker, data-driven vs. values-driven, and people-oriented vs. mission-oriented. Certainly, there are some nonnegotiable features a leader must exhibit—integrity being the most important. Beyond these, however, most leaders need not excel in most of the traits listed in position announcements.

3. Find the Right Balance

More important than any one leadership trait is the ability to adapt your tactics to the situation at hand. The strongly decisive approach that succeeds in case A is likely poorly suited to case B. One faculty member thrives with little direction or oversight, while another needs your constant feedback and guidance. So rather than relying on static leadership strategies, consider different approaches and the tradeoffs they present. Think of your leadership toolbox as filled with a series of seesaws on which you must strike the right balance for the leadership moment. Each seesaw represents a continuum along a single dimension of leadership traits and behaviors. Some challenges and opportunities require you to make choices on a seesaw's far end. Others call for a delicate balance between competing approaches. The seesaw metaphor encourages you to ponder

the spectrum of choices available to you and then to choose those
that promise the greatest success.

4. Engage in Self-Reflection and Solicit Feedback

Striking the right balance on any number of leadership seesaws
requires that you first gain deep self-awareness about your own
preferences, habits, biases, and behaviors. Begin by asking yourself
a series of questions aimed at identifying these patterns. An audit of
your calendar and your past decisions and tactics adds data to con-
firm or undermine your own impressions. Then, request honest
feedback from colleagues, subordinates, and peers. Listen carefully,
and resist feeling defensive when they report impressions of you
that are different from your own. No one is entirely self-aware or
able to perceive their own behaviors as others do. At the same time,
we cannot accurately adjust our own leadership approaches if we
are ignorant of our tendencies and preferences.

5. Deans, Department Heads, and Program Directors Occupy the Space between Faculty and Administration

As members of the faculty who are also leaders and administrators, deans, chairs, and program directors face both the challenges
and opportunities of having feet in both camps. The identity and
role seesaws (chapters 2 and 3) present the dynamics at play in this
especially tricky aspect of academic life.

The challenges emerge especially in institutions suffering under
an "us vs. them" culture. In these cases, faculty and administrators
respectively urge academic leaders to play on their side and against
the other. In such situations, leaders perpetually swim politically
charged waters and often find themselves paralyzed between two
forces who mistrust one another.

In healthier cultures, however, deans and department heads enjoy the opportunity to bridge misunderstandings and perceived differences in constituent interests. They maximize the common interests faculty and administration share. They represent the perspectives of each side to the other. They become the authors of decisions,
actions, and policies that are widely accepted and enduring.

6. Consider Carefully the Type of Leader, Manager, and Decision Maker Your Unit Requires

Seesaws concerning leadership comfort zone, decision-making style, and management style (chapters 4, 5, and 6) all contribute to the myriad choices you make every day as an academic leader, from running a faculty meeting to overseeing a strategic plan. These and everything in between necessitate a broad host of leadership approaches, some of which come naturally while others do not.

Very few department chairs, program directors, or even deans receive any formal training in leadership, decision-making, or management before assuming their post. Yet these are the very essence of your position's duties. Leadership, decision-making, and management are interrelated yet distinct. *Leadership* concerns your abilities to oversee both the unit's daily tasks and its long-term success. *Decision-making* speaks to the extent to which you involve others in decisions large and small. *Management* refers to your supervision of and relationship to the people in your unit. Each merits its own seesaw in this book and in your professional life. They help you avoid the mistakes common to new leaders and require that you become self-aware about your natural inclinations in each area.

7. Your On-Campus and Electronic Availability Are Key to Success

The availability seesaws (chapter 7) examine a profound component of leaders' successes and failures, even while very few take much time to consider it. Your availability—to meet with constituents, respond to email, and be around for an informal chat—intersects directly with your ability to attend to other tasks. In this way, the availability seesaw is especially helpful for effective time management. Use the availability seesaws, both on-campus and online, to strike the proper balance between being readily available and responsive on the one hand, and carving out enough time for your other work. The guiding mantras for a sound availability practice are that your constituents be able to reach you easily and that you respond in the timeframe necessary to address their requests. Outside of these requirements, the availability seesaws provide enormous flexibility in how to manage your time and presence.

8. Your Attention and Your Feedback to People and Behaviors Must Strike Proper Balances

Academic leaders communicate their priorities in the way they manage the attention they give to faculty and staff and in the formal and informal feedback they provide to those same individuals. The attention and feedback seesaws (chapters 8 and 9) walk you through the dimensions to consider in both of these areas: focus on successes vs. failures, frequent vs. rare feedback, and responsiveness to squeaky wheels vs. quieter types. The vast diversity of personality types, behaviors, and performance profiles demands that you be flexible with your attention and feedback practices. Doing so will maximize your communication's effectiveness and, thus, your success as a leader.

ESSENTIAL IDEAS IN THIS CHAPTER

- An effective leader develops the habit of approaching tasks, decisions, and people with a seesaw mindset.
- The seesaws are both individual tools and a habitual way of approaching your professional challenges and opportunities.
- Chapter 1 assesses the culture of higher education today and the many ways it discourages individuals from assuming leadership positions.
- Chapters 2 and 3 help academic leaders navigate the tricky position between "faculty" and "central administration."
- Chapters 4, 5, and 6 aid you in day-to-day decision-making as well as long-term strategic planning. They focus on your self-awareness and choices in your leadership comfort zone, decision-making style, and management style. In each area, you should stretch beyond what comes naturally to embrace styles you will need to draw on.
- Chapter 7 examines availability policies and practices, a crucial yet underappreciated element of a leader's success.
- Chapters 8 and 9 cover how you interact with people, both in day-to-day operations and in performance evaluations. Among the most difficult parts of leaders' responsibilities, human-performance management requires you to be especially self-reflective and adaptable in your approach.

Bibliography

Arreola, Raoul A. *Developing a Comprehensive Faculty Evaluation System: A Guide to Designing, Building, and Operating Large-Scale Faculty Evaluation Systems*, 3rd ed. San Francisco: Jossey-Bass, 2006.

Brown, Tim. *Change by Design*. New York: Harperbusiness, 2009.

Buller, Jeffrey I. *Best Practices in Faculty Evaluation: A Practical Guide for Academic Leaders*. San Francisco: Jossey-Bass, 2012.

Castallo, Richard T. *Dealing with Dysfunction: A Book for University Leaders*. Boulder: Rowman and Littlefield, 2017.

Collins, Jim. *Good to Great: Why Some Companies Make the Leap and Others Don't*. New York: Harper, 2001.

———. *Good to Great for the Social Sectors: Why Business Thinking Is Not the Answer*. New York: Harper, 2005.

Coscarelli, William C. *Decision-Making Style Inventory*, 1st ed. San Francisco: John Wiley and Sons, 2007.

CUPA-HR. "2017–18 Administrators in Higher Education Survey." College and University Professional Association for Human Resources, 2018.

D'Agata, John, ed. *The Making of the American Essay*. Minneapolis: Graywolf Press, 2016.

Eckel, Peter D. *The Shifting Frontiers of Academic Decision Making: Responding to New Priorities, Following New Pathways*. ACE/Praeger Series on Higher Education. Lanham, MD: Rowman and Littlefield, 2006.

Garland, James. *Saving Alma Mater: A Rescue Plan for America's Public Universities*. Chicago: University of Chicago Press, 2009.

Gmelch, Walter H., D. Hopkins, and S. Damico. *Seasons of a Dean's Life*. Sterling, VA: Stylus, 2011.

Gopher, L., L. Armony, and Y. Greenspan. "Switching Tasks and Attention Policies." *Journal of Experimental Psychology: General* 129 (2000): 308–29.

Grazer, Brian, and Charles Fishman. *A Curious Mind: The Secret to a Bigger Life*. New York: Simon & Schuster, 2015.

Heifetz, Ronald. *Leadership without Easy Answers*. Cambridge: Harvard University Press, 1994.

Hersey, Paul, Kenneth H. Blanchard, and Dewey E. Johnson. *Management of Organizational Behavior*, 10th ed. New York: Pearson, 2012.

Jones, LaMont. "Growing Proportion of Part-Time Faculty Portends Problems." *Diverse*, July 11, 2019.

Kahneman, Daniel, Dan Lovallo, and Olivier Sibony, eds. *HBR's 10 Must Reads on Making Smart Decisions*. Cambridge: Harvard Business Review Press, 2013.

Kline, Missy. "The Looming Higher Ed Enrollment Cliff." *Higher Ed Magazine*, 2009.

Kotter, John P. "Management Is (Still) Not Leadership." *Harvard Business Review*, January 9, 2013.

Lederman, Doug. "The Public's Support for (and Doubts about) Higher Ed." *Inside Higher Ed*, June 17, 2019.

Nayar, Vineet. "Three Differences between Managers and Leaders." *Harvard Business Review*, August 2, 2013.

Nocera, Joe. "What Makes Steve Jobs Great?" *New York Times*, August 26, 2011.

Seldin, Peter. *Evaluating Faculty Performance: A Practical Guide to Assessing Teaching, Research, and Service.* San Francisco: Jossey-Bass, 2006.

Yeung, N., and S. Monsell. "Switching between Tasks of Unequal Familiarity: The Role of Stimulus-Attribute and Response-Set Selection." *Journal of Experimental Psychology—Human Perception and Performance* 29, no. 2 (2003): 455–69.

About the Author

Jeanne A. K. Hey, PhD, served as the University of New England's dean of the College of Arts and Sciences from 2011 to 2019. She previously served Miami University for nineteen years in roles including interim dean and executive director of Miami's Middletown Campus, director of international studies, and professor of political science and international studies. A Phi Beta Kappa graduate of Bucknell University, she earned a PhD in political science from the Ohio State University.

Made in the USA
Monee, IL
28 July 2022

10461992R00073